The Case for Character Education

by

Frank G. Goble

and

B. David Brooks

Foreword by

George C. S. Benson

Frank Goble

Green Hill Publishers
Ottawa, Illinois

Copies of this book may be purchased from the publisher for $7.95. All inquiries and catalogue requests should be addressed to Green Hill Publishers, 722 Columbus St., Ottawa, IL 61350. (815) 434-7905.

International standard book number: 0-686-43931-7

Library of Congress Catalogue Card Number: 83-70068

CONTENTS

FOREWORD

"You can't teach ethics." This shallow judgment so often repeated by academicians is completely belied by human experience. Jesus Christ, the Hebrew prophets, Buddha, Confucius, Muhammad, and others have taught ethics with surprising effect. Thoughtful police administrators in Japan have told me that the teaching of Confucian ethics is the most important factor in Japan's great law-enforcement record. Leading educators like the presidents of Harvard and Johns Hopkins are recognizing the need for teaching ethics in America. American medical schools have a course in medical ethics; law schools, some reluctantly, have installed a course in legal ethics in recent years. Harvard now has a Center for Moral Development.

Yet the most important part of our educational system, the public schools, makes only a few real efforts to teach ethics. Some of the reasons for this astonishing gap in education are given in this volume.

Frank Goble and David Brooks have done a splendid job in laying the ghost of "you can't teach ethics." They tell us how important character education is to the maintenance of a decent society. They describe some of the successful efforts to tell youth the reasons for having a decent regard for the rights of our fellows. They briefly sketch the change from revolutionary America's emphasis on ethical idealism to contemporary America's slighting of ethics. Happily and hopefully, they see the pendulum swinging back toward ethical education. This book will help that swinging back to ethics and deserves the reader's careful attention.

Let me add that Great Britain, Japan, West Germany, Sweden, and doubtless other countries, have prepared ethical education materials for secondary or elementary school students. Several other advanced industrial countries have public school courses in "religion," usually interpreted to include ethics. American schools generally do not have such courses; does this shortcoming help explain why our crime rate exceeds that of all these countries? If so, this work is doubly important. It is worth a very careful reading.

George C. S. Benson, Ph.D.
Director, Salvatori Center
President Emeritus
Claremont McKenna College

PREFACE

We Americans are a fortunate people. No other society has achieved such a high degree of freedom and affluence.

Today, however, although our technical achievements are still outstanding, our society is faced with some very disturbing symptoms of social malaise. Chief Justice Warren Burger recently said, "We are approaching the status of an impotent society whose capability of maintaining even elementary security on the streets, in schools, and for the homes of our people is in doubt.... The statistics are not merely grim, they are frightening."[1]

Statistics on juvenile crime are indeed frightening: 31 percent of all violent crimes and 54 percent of property crimes are committed by teenagers; teenage alcoholism has grown to epidemic proportions; marijuana use has increased an estimated 80 percent in three years; suicide is the third leading cause of death for fifteen- to twenty-four-year-olds and has doubled in the last ten years; and more than a million teenage girls become pregnant each year, the majority of them out of wedlock.

This book will identify and document a fundamental weakness in America's overall educational system—the failure of parents, schools, colleges, churches, and other institutions to do an adequate job of teaching character and ethics. The authors are convinced that this weakness is one of the major reasons for presently exploding social problems. In addition, the book will present the case for systematic ethical instruction in our public and private schools as one essential step toward improving the lives of young people and reducing society's social problems.

Although the information in this book is based on nineteen years of research conducted by the Thomas Jefferson Research Center, the subject under discussion is so complex that we found it impossible to cover all aspects of the subject in just this one book. The primary focus is on the essential role that schools—especially elementary schools—can and must play in helping young people develop positive attitudes, goals and values.

I am pleased to have David Brooks as coauthor. David is gaining recognition as one of the leading authorities on youth gangs—one of America's most intractable social problems. His years of experience as teacher and principal have helped to make this volume relevant to the needs and interests of educators.

We are indebted to Anne Montgomery, Hazel Roberts, James Carlton, John Urso, Louise Hughes, James Yates, and other members of the Thomas Jefferson Research Center's staff who have contributed time to this project.

We have started with the premise that all is not well with American society, that current solutions are not solving, and will not solve, exploding human problems, and that there is one American institution that can be exceedingly influential in solving our serious social problems. That institution is the American school system. The schools, which historically functioned in cooperation with the family, church, media, and other institutions to transmit basic cultural values, have in recent years virtually abandoned that role. The thesis of this book is that the schools can and must resume this essential social function.

We will present evidence that systematic character education in American public schools is traditional, permissible, feasible, necessary, and highly beneficial to all concerned.

"Today," correctly states U.S. Secretary of Education Terrel H. Bell, "it becomes more and more imperative than ever for the school system to assume the responsibility for moral education. It stands alone in having both the opportunity and the right to do so."[2]

At present, confusion abounds about character education. Part of this traces to confusion about the meaning of words. It is unfortunate, but nevertheless true, that certain words trigger an emotional response that tends to block discussion of underlying issues.

In the early days of the Republic, words like *virtue* and *enlightenment* were in common use. Jefferson, for example, said, "Virtue is not hereditary."[3] And Benjamin Franklin warned, "Only a virtuous people are capable of freedom."[4]

The word *moral,* although still widely used, often evokes a negative reaction related to censorship and religious dogmatism. Historically, the word *moral* came from the Latin *mos, mores,* and meant "way of life."

The Educational Policies Commission of the National Education Association offers the following definition: "By moral and spiritual values we mean those values which, when applied in human behavior, exalt and refine life and bring it into accord with the standards of conduct that are approved in our democratic culture."[5]

The word *ethics,* derived from the Greek *ethos* ("character"), was once nearly synonymous with morals. In recent years, however, the word *ethics* is often used to describe a formal list of rules—a code of ethics.

Dr. Albert Schweitzer said, "In a general sense, ethics is the name we give to our concern for good behavior. We feel an obligation to consider not only our own personal well being, but also that of others and of human society as a whole."[6]

Values, citizenship, responsibility are other examples of words used to describe correct behavior. Citizenship education usually refers to a broad spectrum of studies including history, law, government, social science, and ethics.

Character, as used in this book, refers to those aspects of personality—mental habits, attitudes, values, personal goals— that influence personal behavior. *Character,* as used in this way, does not include, although it certainly affects, intelligence, special talents or abilities, nor does it include social ethics—ideas about how society should behave (systems of government, economics, etc.).

This definition is clarified by Professor M. G. Bowden: "A person's character is the product of his attitudes, values, goals, objectives, ideals, and habits which influence him to think, feel, and act in certain ways."[7]

Professor Edward A. Wynne, editor of the newsletter, *Character II* says, "The word *character* is often used to describe traits that relate to America's central values. These traits include persistence, tact, self-reliance, generosity, and loyalty."[8]

Linguistic purists may prefer to use *character* to describe one aspect of personality and "ethical instruction" as the means to build character. The authors have often used this approach to the subject.

My own interest in ethical behavior came from many years of experience as a business executive and the gradual realization that, in the long run, ethical behavior really does pay.

In recent years, I have been privileged to know and work with many scholars and educators. This experience has led me to two important conclusions: education is one of the most important tasks that society performs; education is one of the most difficult tasks that society performs.

Frank G. Goble
President
Thomas Jefferson Research Center

Chapter 1

KIDS, CRIME, AND CHARACTER

We are approaching the status of an impotent society
whose capability of maintaining even elementary
security on the streets, in schools, and for the homes of
our people is in doubt.... The statistics are not merely
grim, they are frightening.

Chief Justice Warren Burger

What's wrong with kids today? They just don't seem to know the difference between right and wrong.

This question, so often repeated in school discipline conferences, juvenile court hearings, police stations, and general conversations, came graphically to mind when the nation's newspapers recently reported that thirteen students, perhaps more, drove several miles from school to view the strangled body of a classmate and then failed to report the murder to their parents or to the police.

In reporting this bizarre incident, the local newspaper editorial raised the question as to what there might have been "in the lives of these teenagers that made them simultaneously so willing to participate in that macabre voyeurism and so unable to care."[1]

In Pasadena, California, parents and police were recently stunned by the discovery that eight ten- to twelve-year-old boys in one of the "better" elementary schools were armed with real revolvers and preparing for a gunfight with live ammunition and the intent to kill.

1

Are these examples isolated incidents that can be put aside as just that, onetime occurrences that do not reflect a broader, more widespread social problem? Or are these examples manifestations of a gradual deterioration of our society—symptoms of a society headed for suicide? Do the children of the 80s know the difference between right and wrong?

The new generation of American teenagers, according to a recent article in *U.S. News and World Report,* "is deeply troubled, unable to cope with the pressures of growing up in what they perceive as a world that is hostile or indifferent to them."[2]

One sociologist, according to this report, estimated that one-third of the nation's twenty-seven million teenagers "seem unable to roll with life's punches and grow up lacking the internal controls needed to stay on course."

The problem is not restricted to inner-city youths; it also affects middle-class children reared with every material advantage.

"While there is much public concern with educational matters such as pupil reading scores," states Professor James S. Coleman, "the fact is that the available data disclosed that youth character disorders—as measured by matters such as increased suicide, homicide, and drug use among youth of all races and classes—has become a more profound problem than the decline in formal learning."[3]

Some people are not concerned about the statistics. Young people, they say, have always rebelled against authority. After all, Socrates complained about young people some four hundred years before Christ.

"Our youth," said Socrates, "now love luxury, they have bad manners, contempt for authority, show disrespect for their elders, and love to chatter in place of exercise. They no longer rise when others enter the room. They contradict their parents, they chatter before company, they gobble their food, and terrorize their teachers."[4]

The problem with people who hold this optimistic point of view about youth is that they fail to mention that the youth problems that concerned Socrates eventually led to the decline and fall of the Greek empire.

The fact is, crime and other costly forms of irresponsible behavior are increasing with alarming rapidity and have

2

permeated all aspects of our daily life and social fabric. Our society is staggering under the burden of violence, vandalism, street crime, truancy, teenage pregnancy, business fraud, political corruption, deterioration of family life, respect for others, and the work ethic.

Several surveys of university students taken over the past thirty years have shown that youthful attitudes have veered sharply toward self and away from cooperation with and concern for society. A recently completed major study of affluent, suburban high school students found that "they discount authority, hate school, find it difficult to trust any other human being, and suffer profound malaise from feelings of isolation and lack of purpose."[5]

"Violent Schools—Safe Schools" is the title of a study released several years ago by the National Institute of Education. When HEW Secretary Califano transmitted this report to Congress, he stated, "Schools that should be centers of teaching and learning basic skills and functional literacy have become centers of danger and violence for teachers and students.... The findings of the three-year study indicated that the dimensions of the school crime problem remain extremely serious."[6]

One of the most shocking conclusions from this national survey of elementary and secondary schools was that, "although teenagers spend only 25 percent of their waking hours in school, 40 percent of the robberies and 36 percent of the assaults on teenagers occur in schools. The risks are especially high for youths age twelve to fifteen: a remarkable 68 percent of the robberies and 50 percent of the assaults on youngsters of this age occur in school. Only 17 percent to 19 percent of the violent offenses against youths in this age group occur in the streets."[7]

WHAT IS WRONG WITH KIDS TODAY?

Obviously, something needs to be done about lawless behavior, but what? One of the first steps toward solving any problem is a correct diagnosis of the problem. History provides many examples that illustrate this point.

For instance, in 1854 there was a terrible outbreak of cholera in London. More than five hundred people died within a few weeks. City officials, doctors, and residents tried everything they could think of to stop the epidemic but it continued unabated because they did not know the cause.

John Snow, a local physician who had been studying cholera for years, was convinced that the disease was caused by impure drinking water. He systematically interviewed surviving friends and relatives of victims of the epidemic and found that all the victims had used water from the Broad Street well. Dr. Snow used his research to persuade the guardians of St. James Parish to remove the handle from the Broad Street pump, and the cholera epidemic began to subside.

Crime may be more complex than cholera, but the principle involved is the same: to control crime, we must discover its cause.

Political leaders from both parties now seem to be convinced that the solution for crime and violence is more police, more jails, and longer jail sentences. This implies that lax law enforcement is the cause of crime.

This is a relatively new point of view for many. Until very recently, the "expert" advice of most behavioral scientists— criminologists, sociologists, psychiatrists, psychologists, etc.— has been that punishment is not the answer.

Crime, according to these experts, is a very complex phenomenon caused by environmental factors such as poverty, discrimination, unemployment, and so forth. The widespread academic popularity for this point of view is demonstrated by the fact that it appears again and again in federally financed research studies.

"We have had several major studies of the subject [violence]," writes William H. Blanchard, University of Southern California psychologist, "with the government hiring the best professional talent. The answer is always the same. The cause of violence is injustice. But the correction of social injustice means major social change, so we rush off to order another study."[8]

In December 1969 the National Commission on Violence issued a report on an eighteen-month study based on the research and testimony of more than two hundred leading American scholars. The report says, "The way in which we can make the greatest progress toward reducing violence in America is by taking the action necessary to improve the condition of family and community life for all who live in our cities, and especially the poor who are concentrated in the ghetto slums."[9]

4

In a recent speech, Judge David L. Bazelon of the United States court of appeals in Washington talked of criminal violence in these terms: "Our existing knowledge suggests that the roots of street crime lie in poverty *plus*. Plus prejudice, plus poor housing, plus inadequate education, plus insufficient food and medical care...and perhaps more importantly, plus a bad family environment or no family at all."[10]

The problem with the poverty-causes-crime theory is that it does not fit the facts. Crime and violence have risen to new heights in the United States during the same years in which there has been a decline in poverty and vastly increased expenditures for welfare and education.

Arthur Shenfield, British barrister and economist who has served as a visiting professor at several American universities, states emphatically that poverty does not cause crime. He writes:

> *Suppose that a country has no slums and no depressed ghettos. Suppose that it has no significant racial and religious divisions or conflicts. Suppose that adequate quality of housing is available on assisted terms to all. Suppose that the government redistributes income so that no one is in any dire need. Then if popular views about the causes of crime were well founded, such a country would be almost free from crime. At least it would be free from crime such as robbery, burglary, street mugging and the like, although no doubt some crimes, such as those of passion or sexual deviation, might persist.*
>
> *Sweden is a country with the above-listed conditions. Yet today crime is one of the most striking phenomena of growth in Swedish society. This applies both to crimes of an old-age character, such as robbery, burglary, and street violence, and to newer crimes such as car theft, illegal gambling and bookmaking, dealing in drugs and illicit liquor, and, above all, welfare frauds. So lawless have the cities become that the Stockholm police have been instructed to ignore burglaries, in order to concentrate on grave crimes of violence and on those where the suspect is already in custody. Not only is the crime rate high. It is also*

5

growing fast.... A further related development of ominous proportions is the rise of juvenile delinquency and in particular of acts of vandalism and drug addiction among the young."[11]

LACK OF STANDARDS AS A CAUSE OF CRIME

If poverty and deprivation do not cause crime, what does? Joseph W. Krutch, distinguished American philosopher, gave a simple explanation. "Without standards," he wrote, "society lapses into anarchy and the individual becomes aware of an intolerable disharmony between himself and the universe."[12]

In other words, the root cause of crime, violence, drug addiction, and other symptoms of irresponsible behavior is, for the most part, inadequate or inaccurate ethical instruction. Or, put another way, *responsible behavior must be taught.*

Chief Justice Burger, addressing the American Bar Association about what he called a "reign of terror in American cities," said, "We have established a system of criminal justice that provides more protection, more safeguards, more guarantees for those accused of crime than any other nation in all history." In addition, he said, part of the problem stems from "the fact that we have virtually eliminated from the public schools and higher education any effort to teach values."[13]

The idea that irresponsible behavior is caused by inadequate overall education is consistent with the thinking of some of history's greatest students of human behavior. Confucius, for example, said, "Men possess a moral nature; but if they are well fed, warmly clad, and comfortably lodged without at the same time being instructed, they become like unto beasts."[14]

Modern scholars who support the ethical-ignorance-causes-crime theory may be in the minority, but it is a distinguished and growing minority. Here are some examples:

We seem to have lost sight of one of the primary missions of education—that of transmitting our cultural heritage to our youth.

6

Small wonder that surveys taken over the past thirty years have demonstrated that many of our youth's attitudes have veered sharply toward the self and away from cooperation and the common good.[15]

> *Louis (Bill) Honig,*
> *California Superintendent of Public Instruction*

The biggest failing in higher education today is that we fall short in exposing students to values. Our failure to provide a value framework for young people, who more and more are searching for it, means that universities are turning out potentially highly skilled barbarians.[16]

Steven Muller, Johns Hopkins University President

Every thoughtful person today must be concerned with the state of citizenship education.... As recently as twenty-five years ago, citizenship education, that is, education of the child in morals and civic duty, was the central core and focus of all primary and secondary education. It was what education was about. Thomas Jefferson took for granted that education was citizenship education when he stated his belief that education is indispensable to the working of democracy.[17]

> *John R. Silber, Boston University President*

When we continue to initiate an education system void of standards, void of authority, void of responsibility, void of the ideal, is there really any question as to why the lives of our youth develop lacking moral standards, self-discipline, or a sense of responsibility?[18]

> *George C. Roche, Hillsdale College President*

Dr. John A. Howard, when president of Rockford College and with twenty-five years of experience in college administration, stated emphatically, "The continuing sharp decline among

7

college students in their commitment to the traditional moral values of society ... is, in my opinion, the predictable result of the prevailing philosophy of higher education. It is a philosophy which denies any institutional obligation to provide an understanding of our moral heritage, and which proudly protects those who reject that heritage."[19]

Amoral America is the title of a book by two political scientists, Drs. George C. S. Benson and Thomas S. Engeman. The book is a well-documented summary of the authors' in-depth study of the relationship between crime and ethical instruction. "Our astounding crime rate," the authors conclude, "is largely due to lack of ethics, which, in turn, is due to lack of ethical instruction in the schools and other opinion-forming institutions."[20]

Dr. Engeman continues: *Our thesis is that there is a severe and almost paralyzing ethical problem in this country. Many people dispute this. There are some who do not believe there is a major crime problem; there are some who deny that ethics and crime are related.... We believe that we can demonstrate that unlawful behavior is in part a result of absence of instruction in individual ethics. As political scientists, we have not been merely content to trace the course of the decline in ethical instruction and its correlation with increased crime; we are also interested in analyzing methods by which ethics can be encouraged....*

Contemporary Western society, and especially American society, suffers from inadequate training in individual ethics. Personal honesty and integrity, appreciation of the interests of others, nonviolence and abiding by the law are examples of values insufficiently taught at the present time.... The schools and churches are well situated to teach individual ethical responsibility, but do not do so.[21]

8

In a speech in 1981, Dr. Mark W. Cannon, administrative assistant to Chief Justice Warren Burger, summarized the problem and the solution:

Violent crime and juvenile delinquency have been ascending. Attempts to explain and fight crime have been, at best, only partially successful. The diminished influence of traditional institutions and our failure to promote ethical standards suggest another explanation for crime. Audiovisual media have partially replaced the family, church, school, and community in conveying values to the oncoming generation, and these often appear to encourage hedonism and the use of force. We are in jeopardy of becoming a valueless society and of encouraging decision-making by aggression instead of by reason and democratically established law. If this is the case, then possible avenues to pursue in the prevention and elimination of crime are: teach values in our schools; promote law-related education so young people understand both the rights and the responsibilities of our Constitution and legal system; increase youth activities by constructive organizations; guide children to quality media productions; increase the number of potential bonds or attachments citizens have with prosocial institutions; strengthen families and communities; and educate and constructively counsel delinquents. We must, in short, revitalize and strengthen the moral and ethical foundation of our society.

The possibility of reducing the scourge of crime exists. In addition to skilled, often courageous law enforcement and speedy, just courts, achieving this goal will require devotion, creative energy, and a more widespread commitment to values....

Indeed, the stakes are high. Since decision-making power belongs to the entire citizenry, our system requires widespread responsibility and wisdom. Yet responsibility and wisdom are not ours by nature. They

9

must be learned. If our society neglects this teaching, we do so at our peril....[We] can educate citizens today to civic virtue, moral responsibility, and voluntary support of law. [We] should call their attention to the reasons to abide by the law and to make responsible, ethical contributions to improve our society. Hopefully, this will not only deter law-breaking, but will also enrich the quality of life and happiness of our citizens. May we all rise to the challenge ahead![22]

Chapter 2

IS CHARACTER EDUCATION NEGLECTED?

That moral training is an important part of public school education, no one will deny.... And that it receives all the attention its importance demands, few will affirm.

John Swett,
California Superintendent of Public Instruction
(1863)

Years ago the distinguished scholar John Ruskin said, "The entire object of education is to make people not merely do the right things, but enjoy the right things: not merely learned, but to love knowledge; not merely pure, but to love purity; not merely just, but to hunger and thirst after justice."

Unfortunately, John Ruskin's concept of the purpose of education appears not to be the dominant viewpoint in American schools today. In recent decades, there has been a steady decline in efforts to teach character in our public schools. This decline, we are convinced, is one major reason for the explosive increase in crime, violence, alcoholism, drug addiction, and other disturbing manifestations of moral decay in our society. If this is so, then one of the most effective and economical ways to reduce these problems is to improve the quantity and quality of ethical instruction in all of our institutions, particularly our public schools.

11

In 1967, Sandrah Pohorlak, University of Southern California scholar, made a comprehensive survey of the status of the teaching of moral and spiritual values in the public schools of the United States. She directed a personal letter and questionnaire to the superintendent or commissioner of education in each state, possession, and territory asking how they were treating moral and spiritual values. Of the fifty-five agencies queried, all but six replied, and some of them sent samples of their teaching manuals. The survey revealed that most states mentioned moral education among their educational objectives, although eighteen did not. In spite of this fact, forty-two state departments of education provided nothing in the way of texts, handbooks, or guides to help its teachers teach values; notable exceptions were Florida, Maine, and Alabama.

Mrs. Pohorlak concluded:

> *Here in America, since 1900 or thereabouts, various forces have resulted in the gradual relinquishment of our original standards for morals and ethics, in education, business, and social relationships. . . . There is little or no encouragement from the state offices of education that the districts they preside over be active in finding ways to improve the teaching and encouragement of moral and spiritual values in their school communities.[1]*

Approximately a year after the Pohorlak study was completed, the California Board of Education released a report entitled "Guidelines for Moral Instruction in California Schools" by Edwin F. Klotz. As Mrs. Pohorlak had done, Dr. Klotz also asked the educational leaders in each of the fifty states what they were doing about moral education. His findings were that only thirteen states identified an ongoing program of moral instruction or were in the process of starting one. Four states said they had no committee or guidelines but were interested in what California was doing, and twenty-four states replied that they had neither guidelines nor a committee studying the problem.

Dr. Klotz also surveyed 1,100 California school districts and found that only forty had guidelines or other prepared materials. Seventy-four districts stated that such materials were under preparation, and 447 districts replied that they integrated such instruction throughout the curriculum, but that the instruction was more incidental than direct. Dr. Klotz concluded:

> *The few "guides" we received from out of state we found to be not as well developed as the "moral and spiritual values" guides developed by Ventura and Los Angeles counties.... Most of the guides the California districts submitted were sketchy and did not develop subject matter but usually stated requirements of the law.[2]*

Benson and Engeman provide impressive evidence in their book *Amoral America* that emphasis on ethical instruction has declined in all of our institutions—homes, schools, colleges, media, and even in many churches. Professor Benson states:

> *Until the First World War, ethics was a required course (in addition to chapel attendance) for undergraduates in private liberal arts colleges of denominational background. The texts for these courses can still be found in college libraries.... Although these books vary in their approach to the true ground for ethics— emphasizing first natural law, then passion, then reason—they all share a common concern for improving the character of students.*

> *In today's colleges and universities, the number of students registered in ethics courses in departments of religion or philosophy is small. The method of teaching ethics has also changed since the beginning of the century. This change is partially a consequence of the success of positivism in philosophy. Professors like Rawls, who actually teach about what is ethically good, are rare. Often the professors follow such leaders as Wittgenstein, one of the major proponents of linguistic positivism, who has dismissed ethics as a nonsensical discipline.[3]*

Dr. Benson cites another study, this time about child rearing: "It was observed that the change in the articles written on the subject reflected the change in general intellectual attitudes. The percentage of topics dealing with various aspects of character and/or personality training in three women's magazines was found to be as follows: 1880, 35 percent; 1900, 31 percent; 1910, 39 percent; 1920, 3 percent; 1930, 24 percent; 1940, 23 percent; 1948, 21 percent."[4] Although interest in this subject had declined and then increased again, after 1930 the emphasis was quite different. It had shifted from character development to concern with personality. Problems of adjustment rather than moral problems were emphasized.

In regard to religion, Dr. Engeman says that "organized religion's place in teaching individual ethics is becoming increasingly slight."[5] He continues:

Up until World War II the emphasis on individual ethical responsibility in religious education remained consistently high.... Since World War II, however, the child-centered curricula of the liberal Protestants, Catholics, and Jews have moved away from the old view of Judeo-Christian ethics. Most significantly, they have posited that sin or criminality is not a product of choice but is socially and psychologically determined.[6]

Several surveys show that there has been a dramatic decrease in ethical instruction in American primary schools. Professors De Charms and Moeller, for example, studied fourth-grade readers from 1800 to 1950. They found a substantial decline in moral concern. In 1810, 16 of every 25 pages included moral instruction; by 1930 this had fallen to 1 of every 25, and in 1950 it was .06 of every 25.[7]

Another survey was conducted by Margaret Foster, who analyzed third-grade readers from 1900 to 1953. She found that nonfiction material began to disappear after 1930, as did "obedience and thoughtfulness" and honesty. At the same time, "social activity" and "winning friends" became increasingly important.... Foster concludes that success now depends upon group approval and meeting group standards.[8]

A study made by Parkin of the moral and religious content of

1,291 American school readers from 1776 to 1920, found a 100 percent emphasis on moral and religious content from 1776 to 1786, approximately a 50 percent emphasis from 1786 to 1825, 21 percent in 1825 to 1880, and only 5 percent from 1916 to 1920.[9]

John Nietz made still another study of schools and textbooks, and found that before 1776 religion and morals accounted for over 90 percent of the content of school readers, but by 1926 this was down to 6 percent and in more recent times, too small to be measured. Nietz says that to understand the decline in moral values and the rise in vandalism and crime, we need only contrast the content of the McGuffey Readers with the "literature inflicted on schoolchildren today."[10]

Augustin G. Rudd, in his critique of modern education, *Bending the Twig,* writes: "that only eight of forty-five texts most widely used in sociology courses contend that 'training in moral values' should be stressed in the educational process is a shocking revelation."[11] He points out that character development as a function of public education was influential throughout the nineteenth century but began to disappear in the 1920s.

PREVIOUS WARNINGS

Many scholars have warned us of the severe dangers of a social system that fails to maintain and communicate its system of values, but these warnings have been generally ignored, and our society continues to deteriorate. "The ultimate disease of our time," said Abraham Maslow, the distinguished psychologist, "is valuelessness.... This state is more crucially dangerous than ever before in history."[12]

In December 1940, Walter Lippmann spoke to the annual meeting of the American Society for the Advancement of Science. He said:

> *During the last forty or fifty years, those who are responsible for education have progressively removed from the curriculum the Western culture which produced the modern democratic state. The schools and colleges have, therefore, been sending out into the world men who no longer understand the creative*

15

principles of the society in which they must live.... Prevailing education is destined, if it continues, to destroy Western civilization and is in fact destroying it.[13]

And John Jarolimek, professor of education at the University of Washington, noted:

Increasingly, schools have attended to cognitive learning; that is, basic subject matter and related skills, an area relatively "safe," meaning free of controversy. Schools have steered farther and farther away from affective, moral and values education.... The present emphasis on cognitive learnings with a corresponding lack of attention to affective, moral and values education must be considered a serious shortcoming of American education today.[14]

Warned Bill Honig, California's superintendent of public instruction, "We have a responsibility to pass down and transmit our heritage. Without such transmission, no society can expect to obtain the allegiance of enough of its youth to avoid social disintegration."[15]

In 1966 a survey of a selected cross section of American primary and secondary schoolteachers by the National Education Association Research Division included a question regarding the importance of attempting to develop ethical character in students. Fifty-two percent of the teachers responding believed that too little emphasis was placed on ethical instruction.[16]

WHY IS CHARACTER EDUCATION NEGLECTED?

Reasons for the decline in ethical instruction are complex. Concern for the separation of church and state has undoubtedly been an important factor. Dr. Benjamin Wood, when director of the Bureau for Collegiate Educational Research, Columbia University, some years ago referred to the "lamentable

16

disengagement of American education from its indispensable role in the moral-ethical realm." He said that this disengagement "arose from a grievously erroneous interpretation of the wise separation of church and state, which error in turn grew out of the older and unfortunately still widely accepted error of confusing morality and ethics with one or another specific ecclesiastical affiliation—a basic error which holds that good morals or sound ethics are somehow dependent upon the acceptance of sectarian doctrines and rituals."[17]

Separation of church and state and the legal basis for character education are discussed in Chapter 5.

The increased complexity of society, and thus of education, has been a factor, as has the demand for greater emphasis on technical knowledge. Terrel Bell, U.S. secretary of education, said several years ago:

> *This country's schools were grounded on a concern for transferring our basic values to our children.... In earlier and simpler times this was accomplished through a loose, informal, but intimate confederation of home, church, and school.... Things are not that simple today. The mixed blessings of the industrial revolution, urbanization, technological advances— and all their accompaniments—have led to the highly complex and fragmented social structure we now live in.... Today, then, it becomes even more imperative than ever for the school system to assume the responsibility for moral education. It stands alone in having both the opportunity and the right to do so.[18]*

Another point often made by educators is that if teachers are to be successful in teaching children how to behave, then teachers must receive encouragement and support from the community, parents, legislators, and media—support which has often been lacking.

Dr. Edwin Klotz, in his study for the California Board of Education, concluded: "The schools cannot perform this task [of moral instruction] when beyond the classroom, society is permeated with pictures, films, books, and television programs which tend to undermine the very moral structure the schools are by law required to preserve and revere."[19]

Experts may argue about the influence of the media on youthful attitudes, but few deny that there has been a marked change in the quantity and quality of the media message to young people.

Developing character in young people through the teaching-learning process is a difficult task and one that requires training, patience, tact, and skill. It is easy to see why, as public education has grown into a huge "mass-production" industry with steadily increasing curricular demands, character instruction has suffered.

In discussing why there is a decline in ethical instruction, an article by Dr. Donald Thomas, superintendent of Salt Lake City schools, provides this historical perspective:

> *In the early days moral education was a major part of the school experience. Ethical principles were extracted from the* Bible, Poor Richard's Almanac, *and the basic documents of our nation. Thus, Jefferson urged that high schools stimulate students' minds to "develop their reasoning faculties, enlarge their minds, cultivate their morals, and instill into them the precepts of virtue and order." As for elementary school students, he proposed that they become acquainted with "Grecian, Roman, English, and American history," so they would be adequately informed for participation in community life.*
>
> *Today, however, it is not clear that moral education is fashionable in our schools. It may seem that, in our desire to provide everybody with his "fair share"—and we may call this aim social justice—we have neglected to teach the responsibility of giving, as well as receiving.*[20]

ETHICAL RELATIVISM

The point of view espoused by many academicians is that it is inappropriate to teach ethical concepts because such concepts vary from place to place and time to time. "The objection of the psychologists to the bag of virtues," states one professor, "is that there are no such things."[21]

"In the climate of opinion in which we live," writes Professor David E. Trueblood,

> *particularly in colleges and universities, one of the most popular of all positions is that of ethical relativism. The usual argument runs somewhat as follows: There are many different cultures and civilizations in the world. Each of these has its own orthodoxy about human values, but they are in sharp conflict with one another. Hindus think that it is improper to eat meat or to kill a cow, while Westerners produce cows for the single purpose of killing and eating them. Each group thinks its position is right; therefore, moral values are merely relative to a cultural setting; therefore, moral values are purely subjective; therefore, one is exactly as good as another, for all are lodged merely in human minds and have nothing to do with objective reality.*[22]

Louis E. Raths is coauthor with Merrill Harmin and Sidney Simon of a popular teacher text entitled *Values and Teaching.* "For this writer," states Dr. Raths, "even the idea that we should use all the resources available to us to produce a certain kind of character is repulsive."[23]

> *We believe that each person has to wrest his own values from the available array. . . . We are concerned with the process of valuing and not the product. . . . The method recommends that no moral judgment be made by the teacher, or the child would be robbed of "choice." . . . It should be increasingly clear that the adult does not force his own pet values upon children. What he does is create conditions that aid children in finding values if they choose to do so. When operating with the value theory, it is entirely possible that children will choose not to develop values.*[24]

19

VALUE-FREE SCIENCE

George C. S. Benson says that one reason for the decline in emphasis on ethical instruction has been the First Amendment separation of church and state. "More important, perhaps," he states, "has been the great success of science and its impact on every aspect of our lives.... To measure the impact of scientific positivism on American ethics one could study several major figures, including Darwin, Huxley, Spencer, James, or Sumner, in addition...John Dewey and the psychologists, especially Sigmund Freud."[25]

Benson quotes Freud directly: "Ethics are remote from me.... I do not break my head much about good and evil." "In America," Benson says, "Freud's theories were frequently invoked to minimize punishment as a deterrent and to restrict any kind of ethical instruction."[26]

"Another significant development in psychology," Dr. Benson states,

> *is behaviorism. J. B. Watson, its founder, attempted to make psychology more scientific. He rejected the introspective methods of the Freudians and turned to the more objective and quantitative methods of the biological sciences, arguing that human behavior is the result of conditioned responses to stimuli; e.g., on a simple level, Pavlov's famous dog. In this view, consciousness is either ignored or denied, so ethical choice is replaced by psychological adjustment.*[27]

"Moral and ethical questions," says historian Page Smith, "were increasingly dismissed as 'unscientific.' They were... 'value judgments,' and value judgments were, on the face of it, unscientific. They came out of some archaic religious code and were simply impediments in the way of scientific objectivity."[28]

"Science," stated Dr. Jacqueline Bouhoutsos, former consultant for the Los Angeles County Department of Mental Health, "has traditionally attempted to scrub itself clean from any involvement in morality. Even to hint at a moralistic position was anathema."[29]

Bill Honig wrote an essay titled "The Forgotten Case for

Virtue." He said that there is a simple basic explanation for exploding youth problems—an explanation that is in tune with classical thought, common sense, and the historical experience of most people and societies:

> *This argument, seldom offered because it flies in the face of the reigning intellectual dogma ... is that we are neglecting to place before our youth in a powerful and attractive manner the elevated ethical ideals and expectations of our heritage. More damaging, our antisocial rhetoric has actively devalued the legitimacy of ethical beliefs and emasculated the potency of moral standards. ... Our intellectual classes have abandoned the concept of authority and have abdicated their historical mission of being our ethical guides. ...*
>
> *Several strands have produced the current intellectual consensus of "modernism," which stresses both the freedom of the individual and oppression of society. Daniel Bell, in* The Cultural Contradictions of Capitalism, *and Robert Hogan, in a perceptive article entitled "Theoretical Egocentrism and the Problem of Compliance," delineate the effects of the following intellectual notions: the romantic, Freudian, positivist, Marxist, Rousseauist, egalitarian, and American historical outlooks. Ironically, most of the social, political, economic, and historical circumstances which engendered these movements have substantially changed and robbed these ideologies of their intellectual justification.*[20]

Chapter 3

WHO IS RESPONSIBLE FOR CHARACTER EDUCATION?

All who have meditated on the art of governing mankind have been convinced that the fate of empires depends upon the education of youth.

Aristotle

Most people believe that the family has primary responsibility for developing ethical behavior in the young. Not nearly as well known is the major role that schools played in teaching ethics before 1900. Churches are another important source for ethical instruction and the media too.

Several years ago the Rampart Division of the Los Angeles Police Department made a study of youth gang violence and vandalism. The Rampart Division is in West Central Los Angeles, a densely populated, cosmopolitan inner-city area of diverse economic backgrounds. Approximately ten criminally involved gangs operated in the Rampart area at the time of the study.

The study concluded that lack of discipline within the family structure of many gang-prone youths and a general lack of discipline in community life as a whole significantly contributed to the criminal youth gang problem.

"One obvious answer," the report states,

is to attempt to instill a socially acceptable sense of values in these youths before they reach adolescence.

23

Normally and ideally, this should be accomplished in the family home, but this is often impossible for a variety of reasons, not the least of which is the inadequacy of some parents.

One of the more practical alternatives for developing citizenship (law and order) values in our youth is through the public school system, for that is the system which traditionally responds to the educational needs of our society. It is there that the public school teacher has prolonged contact with the socially disadvantaged student and is in a position to effectively compensate for some of the inadequacies of parental supervision.[1]

A distinguished team of Harvard criminologists, Drs. Sheldon and Eleanor Glueck, studied the lives of more than two thousand delinquents over a period of many years. Their findings are at serious odds with prevailing sociological theories, which place much of the blame for delinquency on poverty and discrimination.

"American criminologists," wrote the Gluecks, "in their preoccupation with sociocultural 'causes' of delinquency and crime, have tended to overlook or minimize the crucial fact that such influences are selective."[2] The Gluecks found that only a small proportion, perhaps 5 to 15 percent, of boys reared in underprivileged areas became delinquents. "Poverty by itself doesn't make a delinquent.... You can find low standards of behavior and neglected children in well-to-do families."[3]

The Gluecks discovered a significant difference between homes of delinquent and nondelinquent children in poor neighborhoods. There were many more criminals and drunkards among the fathers of delinquents. The disciplinary methods of both parents were far less adequate than those in the homes of nondelinquents, and delinquents more often came from broken homes.

"What is really required," they stated, "is great firmness administered with love.... Love is the essential element.... Clearly we must not neglect the fact that it is the emotional poverty, the spiritual poverty, as well as the actual physical poverty that must be recognized."[4]

24

More recently, Richard H. Blum, an American psychologist, published *Horatio Alger's Children,* a book about the role of the family in the origin and prevention of drug risk. The book describes the work of a research team headed by Dr. Blum which made a three-year study of almost a thousand middle-class parents and children. The researchers conclude that children of permissive parents have a far greater chance of becoming hooked on hard drugs than those whose parents are strict but affectionate. Blum writes:

> *As scientists we were surprised to find that the best protection a child can have against drugs is the old-fashioned group of moral virtues.*
>
> *Families that believe in God and country, went to church regularly, loved their children but disciplined them strictly and respected the police were not bothered with a drug problem.*
>
> *But families that believed children must be free to "find themselves," that practiced no religion or very little, and that mistrusted or were disrespectful to authority generally had youngsters who took to drugs.[5]*

THE CHANGING AMERICAN FAMILY

It seems obvious that many families today are significantly different from the family of thirty or fifty years ago, and this difference has had a profound effect on the teaching of basic values to children.

Generally, a child born into a pre–World War II family could look forward to a fairly stable environment with parents who molded the child's character through interpersonal relationships. There would be a mother and father, and they would be the same two people throughout the childhood and adolescence of the child. And there would probably be four grandparents, several aunts, uncles, cousins, and a number of brothers and sisters. For the most part, this was the rule rather than the exception. A relatively small number of divorces took place—unlike current trends, which indicate a divorce rate of over 50 percent of all marriages.

In addition to this family constellation, there would be a relatively small number of persons who had influential contact with the child during the formative years. They might include a handful of teachers; a priest, minister, or rabbi; local merchants; neighbors; and, of course, the peer group.

All in all, the number of persons important to a youth's early and teen years probably did not exceed thirty people. Additionally, this small number of persons was likely to be fairly homogeneous; that is, because they spent time together, lived and worked near each other, and went to neighborhood schools, they generally held similar beliefs.

There were other influences apart from this group, such as movies, comics, radio, theater, newspapers, books, and magazines. However, by and large, the pre–World War II child had a close circle of persons who influenced character development and was not bombarded by an extensive array of conflicting models from other persons or sources.

Following World War II, significant changes began to take place within and around the American family. The war took families from the farms and put them into the large industrial cities of the nation. A nation that was once fairly immobile became highly mobile, and with this mobility came a subtle but significant change in the family. Families once living in close proximity found themselves spread over the continent.

With this mobility also came the growth of the tract home and the moving together of people with diverse ethnic, religious, and personal backgrounds.

As mobility increased, new pressures were placed on the family. Women who had to work during the war effort continued to work; the number of mothers in the work force steadily increased through the late 1940s into the 1950s and has continued into the 1980s. This further changed the structure of the family and introduced children to a variety of persons who took care of them while their parents were at work.

Gradually, it became obvious that the baby boom and the accelerated divorce rate were beginning to have an effect on the American family. The baby boom brought on new pressures, and the divorce rate resulted in a shift in the makeup of the family and the influence that parents exerted over the character development of their children.

These changes during the past thirty years have greatly altered the structure of the family and its ability to transmit ethical standards to the next generation.

CHANGING CONCEPTS OF CHILD REARING

In addition to the formidable changes in the makeup of the family, there was a shift in concepts of child rearing. The same intellectual theories that influenced formal education also influenced many parents. Parents, like schools, became more permissive, and emphasis shifted from individual responsibility to social responsibility—a don't-blame-yourself point of view.

The idea that crime and violence were the fruit of forces outside the individual—poverty, lack of education, etc.— resulted in a decrease in the emphasis that many parents put on teaching personal responsibility to their children. The forces that caused crime were thought to be beyond the control of parents, and thus not their responsibility.

Paul Roazen, an authority on Freud, stated that in child rearing, "There was a time in the history of psychoanalytical doctrine when the inclination was to view all suppression as negative, all controls of the child as hindrances to his development."[6]

Richard Blum, based on his studies of the relationship between parenting styles and drug abuse, found that low-risk parents were confident leaders and their children seemed to have strong leadership qualities too. High-risk parents, influenced by modern value-free behavioral theories, were opposed to strong leadership. Dr. Blum says:

If there is no final authority, if all things are relative, and if man's mind is the highest form of life, the ultimate responsibility of the individual as well as anguish are the results. High-risk parents have accepted, as their ethic, the most spectacularly

27

successful enterprise of this century—the positivistic, pragmatic, scientific model [value-free science of which Dr. Abraham Maslow was so critical]. . . . If parents are not buttressed by traditional moral standards based on a faith in the order of things, they can only rely— insofar as they might wish to counter such hedonism at all—on arguments drawn from a new faith in pragmatism and science.[7]

Dr. Blum and his colleagues discovered not only that children raised to respect traditional values were less apt to suffer from drug abuse problems but also that they and their families were happier. Happiness and pleasure within the family circle were characteristic of low-risk families—pain and humiliation were inflicted in high-risk families. "Youth who suffer no drug risk," writes Dr. Blum, "have discovered that the values worth living by are self-respect and respect for others and kindness and responsibility to the family and to oneself."[8]

THE CHURCH AND CHARACTER

Organized religion, most people will agree, has played an important part in influencing ethical conduct.

Russell Hill, a retired business executive, studied the ethical concepts of major world religions and concluded that there was general agreement on such ethical concepts as: courage, conviction, generosity, kindness, helpfulness, honesty, justice, tolerance, sound use of time and talents, freedom, and good citizenship.

Several studies of religion in America have shown that a high percentage of Americans are religious. One Gallup poll, for example, estimated that 94 percent of adult Americans believe in God.[9]

Unfortunately, as Benson and Engeman found in their study of religious school curricula, many churches have significantly reduced their former emphasis on individual ethics. Professor Engeman writes:

The modern church . . . has, to a large extent, modified its concern with individual ethics. Judeo-Christian

28

ethics has been replaced in the churches' interest by social action and psychological views of individual happiness. In so doing, the churches have followed the intellectual theories coming from the society around them—particularly from the universities. According to these views, individual unhappiness and criminality are consequences of social forces, and are not questions of spiritual or ethical choice. As long as there is racism, militarism, economic exploitation, etc., one should not be surprised—the argument goes—to find criminal reactions to these conditions....

Freud and other psychologists-psychiatrists have... had a powerful influence on church men. If criminals are created by early childhood experience or other environmental influences, then it is superfluous to talk about ethical standards and individual responsibility.[10]

Dr. Engeman says that in spite of a large number of studies, the results are inconclusive as to whether religious conviction does modify delinquent behavior. He quotes a 1961 study by Travers and Davis summarizing the existing studies as follows: "Findings are in complete conflict and range from those investigators who view religion as a cure to those who seem to view it as a cause."[11]

THE MEDIA TAKE THEIR TOLL

It might be reasonable to assume that the changes in the family brought about by permissive child-rearing practices, mobility, divorce, and the influence of relativistic science would not have had such a great impact were it not for the power of the media. Where it is reasonable to think of a child thirty or fifty years ago as being shaped by twenty to thirty influential persons, it is now plausible to consider that thirty to fifty different people, with a wide range of ethical points of view, influence a child each day through television.

It would be inaccurate to label television the sole "cause" of the disturbing growth of crime and violence in American society. Nevertheless, it would be irresponsible to overlook the influence of television on the American family as a powerful factor in the character development of young children and the lessening of parents' power to influence that development.

Supporting this point of view, Fredric Wertham, consulting psychiatrist at Queens General Hospital in New York, states in his article, "School for Violence, Mayhem in the Mass Media":

> *If somebody had said a generation ago that a school to teach the art and uses of violence would be established, no one would have believed him. He would have been told that those whose mandate is the mental welfare of children, the parents and the professionals, would prevent it. And yet this education for violence is precisely what has happened and is still happening; we teach violence to young people to an extent that has never been known before in history.* [12]

He then cites an example:

> *Recently,* Jack the Ripper *was shown on television eight times in one week, at times particularly available to children and young people. On Saturday it was shown at noon, immediately after a program specifically addressed to children. On Sunday it was shown twice in the time between 11:30* a.m. *and 3:30* p.m. *The different showings were followed by a promotion spot showing the killing of four police officers.* [13]

Numerous studies support the fact that the influence of the media results in a value system that idealizes violence as good, as an acceptable solution for problems, and as a means of winning.

Shortly after twenty-eight-year-old David Radnis saw the movie *The Deer Hunter* on television, he killed himself playing Russian roulette. At least twenty-eight other people shot themselves in a similar way after viewing the movie. [14]

A federally financed study, released in May 1982 by the National Institute of Mental Health, concluded that "violence on television does lead to aggressive behavior by children and teenagers who watch the programs." The report mentioned one

30

five-year study of 732 children that found that "several kinds of aggression—conflicts with parents, fighting, and delinquency—were all positively correlated with the total amount of television viewing."[15]

Some social scientists believe that television exerts more power, and is probably a faster and more efficient teacher, than parents, thus reducing the effect that parents have in their efforts to teach or model appropriate character traits.

The influence of television is summarized by Wertham:

> *Children have absorbed and are absorbing from the mass media the idealization of violence. Not the association of violence with hate and hostility, but the association of violence with that which is good and just—that is the most harmful ingredient. We present to children a model figure to emulate and model method to follow. The model figure is the victorious man of violence. The model method is the employment of violent means. The hero's reasoning is usually only a gimmick; his violent action is very real. The child who sits down to view one of his ubiquitous Westerns or similar stories can be sure of two things: there will be foul play somewhere, and it will be solved by violence. The ideal is not the pursuit of happiness, but the happiness of pursuit.... Children do not learn from these shows that "good guys win over bad guys"; rather, they learn that violence is exciting—and, since we allow so much of it to be shown to them, that it is probably a pretty good thing.*

> *You cannot teach morals in a context of violence. The nonviolent moral is lost in the violent detail.*[16]

HOME VS. SCHOOL: WHO SHOULD TAKE THE LEADERSHIP?

Because of changes in the family, high mobility, the influence of the media, and the instability of the child's environment, we can no longer argue that the home—or, as others say, the home

31

and church—is the only place where character education should take place.

Nevertheless, many people remain convinced that the home, not the school, is the institution properly responsible for ethical instruction. For example, when Sandrah Pohorlak asked state superintendents what they were doing about teaching values, one state superintendent replied that the home alone has the responsibility of teaching moral and spiritual values.[17] The unfortunate result of this line of reasoning is that when parents fail—as they too often do—society must pay the bill.

Several years ago, Congressman Charles E. Bennett told a congressional committee on education that "the home and the church can no longer be solely relied upon. Today they are least available when most needed. These institutions today are no longer equipped to handle the job without help from our schools. Those children who are most in need of instruction are getting it least."[18]

Richard Gorsuch, professor of psychology at George Peabody College for Teachers, has conducted extensive research regarding student values and their origins. He told an American Education Research Association conference that teachers were found to play a major role in value development for elementary school children.[19] He also cited previous research by Bronfenbrenner that suggested that "the adult who spends the greatest amount of time in significant interaction with the child is likely to have the most influence." His examination of our culture suggests that teachers may spend more time in "significant interaction" with children than do their parents.[20]

The fact is, until sometime shortly before 1900, character building was believed to be an essential part of the formal educational process at all levels.

Without doubt, since education in America became public toward the middle of the nineteenth century, ethical instruction has been handicapped by accurate and inaccurate interpretations of the First Amendment separation of church and state. Nevertheless, in the early days of public education, the majority of educators continued to believe that moral instruction was an important part of their task.

Horace Mann (1796-1859) was one of the prime movers in creating the American system of free public education. He

32

believed that education should be universal, nonsectarian, and free, and that its aim should be social efficiency, civic virtue, and character rather than mere learning for the advancement of sectarian ends. [21] In 1916 John Dewey wrote, "It is a commonplace of educational theory that the establishment of character is a comprehensive aim of school instruction and disciplines."[22] Students of educational history, however, report that Dewey fell under the spell of relativistic behavioral science and that his enthusiasm for character education waned in his later years.

Over a hundred years ago (1863), John Swett, a famous superintendent of public instruction for California, said, "That moral training is an important part of public school education, no one will deny.... And that it receives all the attention its importance demands, few will affirm."[23]

TEACHERS HAVE ENDORSED CHARACTER EDUCATION

In 1918 the Commission on Secondary Education, appointed by the National Education Association, issued what is perhaps the most historic statement ever made on the goals of public education. The statement has since been called the "Seven Cardinal Principles of Education." The principles were (1) health, (2) command of fundamental processes, (3) worthy home membership, (4) vocation, (5) citizenship, (6) worthy use of leisure, and (7) ethical character.[24]

In 1954 the National Education Association Representative Assembly adopted the following resolution:

> *The National Education Association recognizes the necessity for a clear understanding of fundamental moral and spiritual values.* The Association believes, that along with the home, the church, and the community, the school has a major responsibility for building this understanding into human behavior. [*Emphasis added*]
> *The Association recommends that teacher education institutions and in-service programs stress consistently*

33

the methods through which these values may be developed and urges continuing research to increase effectiveness of instruction in moral and spiritual values.[25]

Another NEA memo, this one issued by the organization's Research Division in November 1963, stated:

After the establishment of the principle of separation of church and state, the tenets of specific religious groups could not be represented in public schools. Nevertheless, it has always been believed that even without a sectarian emphasis, the public schools can and should teach the moral and social ideals of conduct which contribute to harmonious human relations.[26]

In 1965, wondering if the previously mentioned 1918 goals were outmoded, the NEA conducted a teacher survey. The teachers surveyed returned an overwhelming verdict in favor of the seven cardinal principles: 85 percent of them said these principles were still a satisfactory list of major objectives in education. The teachers did not believe, however, that all principles were being given sufficient emphasis. The three greatest deficiencies mentioned were the worthy use of leisure, worthy home membership, and ethical character.[27]

Thus, educators have repeatedly recognized ethics as an important area for instruction. Unfortunately, as we have previously discussed, a wide gap exists between recognition of the need and effective implementation in most schools.

"Today," correctly states Secretary of Education Terrel H. Bell, "it becomes more and more imperative than ever for the school system to assume the responsibility for moral education. It stands alone in having both the opportunity and the right to do so."[28]

Chapter 4

IS CHARACTER EDUCATION FEASIBLE?

Education makes a greater difference between man and man than nature has made between man and brute. The virtues and powers to which men may be trained, by early education and constant discipline, are truly sublime and astonishing.

John Adams

Many people are skeptical about the feasibility of direct, systematic character education. Some say that it cannot be done, others believe that character is "caught but not taught," and a third point of view is that it cannot be taught without reference to religion.

Dr. Max Rafferty, when he was state superintendent of education in California (1968), said, "Never until this time, to my knowledge, has any formal attempt been made to try to set up a code of ethics or morality, which by necessity has to be pretty largely separated from any sectarian religious bodies. I am not sure it can be done."[1]

The purpose of this chapter is to show that when correct methods are used, one can successfully teach basic ethical values in the public school.

Dr. Herbert Mayer, former president of American Viewpoint, an organization that spent more than fifty years studying juvenile delinquency, said, "It has often been said that values cannot be taught directly. This assumption has been the cause of much

35

failure.... The unrestrained freedom and irresponsibility so prevalent in the present generation of children and young people is ample evidence for the result of this kind of education."[2]

He cited the investigations of delinquents conducted by Drs. Sheldon and Eleanor Glueck of Harvard University. Their research reveals rather conclusively, he said, that there is little correlation between delinquency and family income or general environmental influences. The majority of young people growing up in poor neighborhoods, they discovered, did not become delinquents, whereas children coming from what appeared to be excellent environments sometimes did become delinquents. "Prevention of delinquent careers," wrote the Gluecks, "as our findings suggest, is dependent upon something more specific than the manipulation of general cultural environment. It entails the structuring of integrated personality and wholesome character during the first formative years of life."[3]

Scholars opposed to systematic ethical instruction often cite the work of Professors Hugh Hartshorne and Mark May (1928–30). Their studies failed to produce any positive evidence that character education classes conducted by schools, churches, or the Boy Scouts caused better behavior.[4]

In 1940, Professors Robert Peck and Robert Havighurst, dissatisfied with the method used by Hartshorne and May, undertook a new study. Their extensive studies of schoolchildren over a period of sixteen years led to more optimistic conclusions. Character, they found, was definitely learned.

"Since character structure," they state,

> *and even specific, detailed ways of acting, appear largely learned by emulation of the attitudes and behavior of those few people who are emotionally essential to the growing child, it seems evident that moral preaching which is not backed by consonant behavior is largely a waste of time and effort. Indeed, it may often be worse than useless if it teaches children to say one thing and do another.... Children do as we do, not as we say. Their character tends to be an accurate reflection of the way their parents act toward them.[5]*

THE GOOD AMERICAN PROGRAM

To test the feasibility of schools teaching character, American Viewpoint* devised a teacher's manual, *The Good American Program*. This manual was adopted in Ossining, New York, for students from kindergarten through sixth grade. The program combined the teaching of ethics with social studies.

Initially, the Ossining experiment was highly successful, and administrators and teachers reported improved student deportment. On one occasion when supervision was interrupted by the death of a staff member, the teacher committee asked the superintendent of schools for his consent to go ahead with the program. Unfortunately, after several years the program began to lose momentum as new administrators, unfamiliar with the program, took office.

Shortly after the character education experiment began in the Ossining public schools, a group of parents representing both Christian and Jewish religions objected on the grounds that the schools were in violation of the First Amendment. School officials invited the parent group to examine the lesson material carefully and observe teachers using it in the classroom. After the investigation the group withdrew their objections.

THE CHARACTER RESEARCH PROJECT

The Character Research Project of Union College, Schenectady, New York, under the direction of Ernest Ligon, has spent many years seeking ways to develop character. This organization's carefully documented research offers additional evidence that the character of young people can be systematically developed. Dr. Ligon stated emphatically, "Character is taught, not caught."

One of the organization's experiments, conducted in cooperation with Park Preparatory School in Indianapolis,

---

* This organization is still active but has changed its name to Ethics Resource Center and moved its headquarters from New York City to Washington, D.C.

involved seventy-four boys enrolled in grades five through eight. The study sought to determine whether direct character instruction would modify behavior more than indirect teaching. Detailed statistical analysis indicated that the direct instruction was much more productive.[6]

AS I AM, SO IS MY NATION

In Colton, California, Virginia Trevitt became deeply concerned about national trends in juvenile delinquency and the behavior of students in her school. Her concern led her to the development of a course of study with the theme As I Am, So Is My Nation.[7] Her aim was to "create a new type of student who sees education as relevant to the needs of the world; to equip the individual with the moral qualities needed to make his best contribution to his generation."

The course was accepted by the board of education and her high school principal, and she was authorized to teach it to all incoming freshmen. Her methods were lecture, discussion, and experimentation. She offered her students a chance to study the ideas and ideals of the Founding Fathers.

The course changed the lives of hundreds of students, who developed new pride, purpose, and enthusiasm, and for three years running Colton High School won the coveted Freedom Foundation Award. Mrs. Trevitt reports the following results:

> *Many students returned stolen articles when they understood the relevance of their petty thefts to the graft in high places in the nation. Boys put things right with employers they had cheated, and parents to whom they had lied. Others assumed responsibilities at home and at school they had been evading. Students stopped cheating in classes when they realized the relation of personal integrity to the gross forms of dishonesty in the nation.*

> *A student strike was pending against a substitute teacher they said they hated. Some students, whose orientation to this new kind of world order had become*

38

clear, were able to convince the strikers that strikes were divisive and destructive. Within an hour they had found a better solution. Subsequently, the teacher said the class was totally different.

In many homes family life was affected dramatically. Students told of new appreciation of their parents and new respect for brothers and sisters. Duties at home took on surprising meaning when we studied how sound homes could become real arsenals of democracy. Parents came to school confirming their experiences and wrote letters saying, "Something has happened to our child!"[8]

TEACHING CHILDREN TO CARE[9]

Dorothy Kobak is a psychiatric social worker with the New York City schools. She was concerned with the deterioration of ethical values in our society, as evidenced by crime and other forms of maladaptive behavior. She believed that schoolchildren should and could be taught to care for others. Her Teaching Children to Care project was aimed specifically at testing ways to help children develop their "caring quality" at Public School 9, the Walter Reed School, in New York City. This was a special school where students continued their education in separate facilities from the mainstream of pupils because of their disturbed behavior.

The goal of the project was to test whether the caring quality could be "taught." The plan was to utilize every class experience or individual student experience that would illustrate a moment of caring or lack of caring. These moments could occur during class lessons, between lessons, or in specific talk times when problems relating to caring would be discussed.

The majority of students at Walter Reed School came from very low-income and broken homes. Ethnically, they were from minority backgrounds. Everything in their family and social environment fought against growth experiences. Their common needs stressed individual survival and this was not conducive to caring for others. Their parents also faced the problem of

39

survival in a climate where to "care" was dangerous—either you were overpowered or ridiculed.

The Care project operated on the premise that teachers should not write off the potential capacity of emotionally disturbed or socially maladjusted students to learn and grow. This was vital because these students had written themselves off. The process of talking up instead of down to the students was a sign of respect that prompted great striving by them to live up to the expectations of the therapist or teacher. It was a challenge they welcomed.

The project used specific creative techniques as a springboard for discussions—videotape, psychodrama, poetry, clay modeling, round-robin storytelling, and pantomime. It was felt that with this particular school population, inexperienced in verbalization, indirect methods of expression were more appropriate and meaningful.

Many subjects occasioned dialogues—truancy, stealing, fighting, and so forth. But all the discussions focused on the lack of caring for self, each other, society, or life in general. Any discussions on morality or doing "wrong" or their consequences were avoided. Instead, the focus was on empathy, sympathy, compassion, concern, or altruism.

Dr. Kobak offers the following example of the teaching process:

One psychodrama revolved around an experience that took place in a classroom and was later re-enacted to stimulate a new response. During a classroom discussion with fifteen-year-old boys, a young ten-year-old entered the classroom with a note. Nobody knew him but he was called ugly names, booed, hissed, derided, humiliated, and degraded. The conduct was completely unprovoked. Of course, these were their unconscious expressions of the power principle for which they strived and the manifestation of a defense system geared to ward off threat. Here was a spontaneous situation where ego gratification was instant, complete, and totally satisfying. But the most damaging factor was the reality that the young boy was totally demolished. He did not understand why he

40

warranted their hostility, but he learned quickly he had better imitate this in order to survive! He immediately retaliated in kind, but with fear and without enthusiasm or rationale other than to feel safer in a bewildering situation. Here lies the tragedy! Had the older boys given him a different response of welcome or fellowship, he would have had a new growth model to emulate. Also, the older boys, by being the catalyst, would reinforce their own caring quality.

After the young boy left, the class re-enacted the scene in psychodrama on videotape with one of the fifteen-year-old boys taking the part of the ten-year-old. The class was instructed to react with friendship when the "young boy" entered the room. The whole class erupted with "Hi, man! Cool, man! What's your name?" There was jumping up and backslapping and palmslapping. They observed themselves on video, enjoyed their image, and were subtle recipients of an input opportunity *of positive programming. This was followed up with dialogue which touched on concepts such as empathy, self-esteem, and being an example to others. This gave them a primary gain of self-importance since they never conceived that they could ever be positive models. In addition, this started a process of building a sense of awareness for the future by establishing an experimental positive recall that was satisfying. Hence, an automatic desire was established to repeat the pleasurable feedback.*

Response to videotape was excellent. It appeared that seeing oneself in instant, on-the-spot feedback was an ideal, immediate, total verification not only that "I am Somebody Real" there on the screen but, indeed, "I AM at all!"

Using a popular rock-folk song, "El Condor Pasa" ("I'd Rather Be a Hammer Than a Nail"), students were asked to state what they "would rather be." They mentioned, "I'd rather be the bat than the ball"; "I'd rather be the hook than the fish"; etc. They had to verbalize their reasons and eventually were involved in a discussion of sadness which they felt was the end result of being in a weak position. After discussing how they could recognize when a person was sad, they were then given a piece of clay and asked to "make" the word "sad." The boys worked with intensity and introspection, their faces and fingers being videotaped while they worked. For boys who could not sit still, who were prone to destroy rather than create, this was an excellent verification of their capacity for involvement and the reward of success (a completed project), plus a means of self-expression that was not only acceptable then but later deemed helpful to the peers around them.

The Care project did not lend itself easily to statistical analysis. Teachers who used the program, however, said that a formal program to teach children to care restored their excitement and hope for their profession. Small successes became milestones. Students shared their candy more readily. They held doors open for adults behind them. They apologized for fighting or taking possessions away. They expressed greetings and thanks with much more frequency and warmth. All of these manifestations formerly had represented great risks for ridicule or lack of reward.

Those involved with the Teaching Children to Care project reached three conclusions:

1. It is desirable to teach children to care!
2. It is possible to teach children to care!
3. It is essential to teach children to care!

"So much clinical and educational training," wrote Dorothy Kobak,

> is focused on understanding and curing the negative: crime, drug addiction, alcoholism, mental illness, etc. Yet, little is done academically in universities, in formally studying principles and techniques of "health" and its maintenance in the manner of Sorokin, Montagu, and Maslow. Even less is offered students of education in teacher training programs to develop skills toward character education which many students are voicing as consistent with the definition of their role

*as academic teachers, particularly since so many years
are spent in school, and teachers have so much access to
children in the formative years.*

BUILDING CHARACTER IN A HARLEM SCHOOL[10]

Frances Lou Taylor was a new white teacher in a black Harlem school. Her black friend and former supervisor Melissa urged that she start the school year with a tea for the parents. "Without it," she declared, "you're lost. If you do it, you'll have the whole year made!" And that made sense, for a child's prime teachers are its parents.

The very first hour, Frances told her thirty-four black and white fifth-grade Harlem children that all the work they did the first week would be discussed with their parents at a tea scheduled for the first Friday of the school year. Parents who could not come, she said, would get the children's work through the mail.

The children got down to business and put forth their best efforts the whole week. They decorated the room with their best drawings, drew a welcome sign and put it over the door, and delivered an invitation to the principal. The teacher brought and borrowed cups, made cake. The children hosted their parents: hung up their coats, served tea, learning manners and respect. Parents who had been belligerent simmered down. Each child got a piece of cake. And the teacher gave the parents her home phone number and invited them to call whenever necessary. (This number was not used too much, yet gave a sense of *in*ness.) The teacher showed them what the state requires and asked them what *they* wanted besides, so they could make part of the curriculum. And she gave them the next week's work assignment so they could help the children off to a good start.

Each morning and afternoon fights would break out. Frances found out that most of the children usually came to school hungry. So she bought cocoa and bread for all of them, to start the day. Just to get them into working condition took major effort every morning. In the process, the children learned to

43

measure cocoa, water, milk; to keep records of carbohydrates, proteins, etc.; to care for kitchen equipment.

In the depressed Harlem section of New York City thirty percent of the youth are unemployed. Discouragement and insecurity press on many people beyond bearing. Teachers are frequently beaten, shot, stabbed, and raped; vandalism and theft are at their fearful peak; children are robbed, sometimes wantonly maimed. It was in these conditions that Frances rallied some of the parents and children to turn the trend in her class.

The male teacher in the next room and Frances separated fighters and took in each other's toughest fighting children to cool off. She had a beat-up round table in the back of the room which she and the children had covered with a pretty flower-patterned plastic sheet. A child would stomp in, throw himself in a chair, shouting four-letter curses till she could get him or her calmed down and doing something interesting. At any moment another would come in and upset the class again; and then another and another, every day. And the first eight weeks there were no books, notebooks, pencils, chalk; no school supplies. Frances bought as many as she could, and wrote to friends back home to send her what they could collect.

Their classroom hadn't been painted for twelve years. (The school had been built in 1901: a five-floor walk-up, and her class was on the top floor.) It was a bilious green, dark and dirty. In such surroundings the children were, of course, very destructive. And she knew unless they made the room theirs, they would break it and her down together. So on the first Friday morning, before the tea, she told them that all boys who could come were needed to help paint the classroom the next morning.

The boys who showed up on Saturday to paint the classroom were deemed a menace by the storekeepers and were routinely chased away. The two painters whom Frances had hired took them to the hardware store and introduced them to the storekeeper as boys who were helping them to paint their classroom. They showed the boys how to compare qualities and prices of paints and brushes; to add up the figures and count the change. The store owner was so pleased that he gave them painters' caps, which the boys loved and which (as it turned out) gave them prestige with their comrades.

On Monday morning they and their classmates were dazzled

44

by their white school room, the most beautiful in the whole school.

Before the room was painted the janitor had left the floor as dirty as the children kept the walls and ceiling. Now he was so pleased that he lugged his heavy machine up five flights of stairs and polished the floor beyond the call of duty. Besides that, he routinely cleaned up the pellets left here and there by the pet rabbit, which hopped about the room chewing the remains of bubble gum and stopping to be scratched.

Previously, nobody cared what happened to the dingy room, so it got dirtier all the time. But now if a child happened to run his hand across a wall and leave a mark, others would shrilly point it out and he would quickly clean it off, keeping it nice for everybody.

The principal praised the class at the school assembly and urged the others to emulate Frances's students. He showed their classroom off to visitors, and that made the children keep it even more neat and clean. The students developed responsibility: they organized an animal-care committee for their rabbit, gerbils, and the baby rat that came out every day and warmed itself on the electric plug; and a plant-care committee.

The supervisor of student teachers (Professor Florence Katz) sent her student teachers impartially all over the school. But more of them chose Frances's class than any other, helping it in many unusual ways. One, for example, was a shy young man who could focus on objects better than on people. He thought of making a wire cage to protect the rabbit from the cat-sized rats that at night devoured gerbils and other animals housed in wooden cages. He got ten boys to do something that interested them: measuring, arithmetic, drawing, shopping, finally building.

Toward the end of the school year some parents gave Frances a surprise chicken dinner: they served it to her in the classroom. The children stood around in a delighted circle, watching her eat this ceremonial meal of thanks.

After Frances left the school, some of the children spontaneously formed a mutual-help group. When one of them was getting into trouble, others would tell Frances about it and take that one to her for counseling.

THE CHARACTER EDUCATION CURRICULUM

Demonstration projects—such as the one just described—are not convincing to most social scientists, who point out that without a control group, one cannot be sure that the results are genuine. People involved in experimental projects, they say, often become emotionally involved and lose their ability to be objective.

Another problem is that programs like those developed by Virginia Trevitt, Dorothy Kobak, and Frances Taylor succeed because their originators are deeply concerned and committed and, in addition, are highly talented individuals.

There have been a number of attempts to develop programs that can be widely used by "average" classroom teachers. It is not possible for the authors to describe all of these programs or provide any guide to their relative effectiveness. One program with which the authors are very familiar is the Character Education Curriculum; it was developed by the American Institute for Character Education in San Antonio, Texas, and is distributed by the American Institute and the Thomas Jefferson Research Center.

Russell C. Hill, founder of the American Institute for Character Education, based the program on a worldwide study of value systems. The study identified fifteen basic values shared by major world religions and cultures. The values are: courage, conviction, generosity, kindness, helpfulness, honesty, honor, justice, tolerance, the sound use of time and talents, freedom of choice, freedom of speech, good citizenship, the right to be an individual, and the right of equal opportunity.

The program is organized so that there is a teacher's kit for each grade level from kindergarten through sixth grade. Each kit contains an explicit teacher's manual, colorful wall posters, student activity sheets, and evaluation forms.

Completed in 1970, the Character Education Curriculum was tested in four hundred schools in several states with varied racial and economic level students.

This program is now used in over seven thousand classrooms across the country. In some instances, this approach has produced rather dramatic improvements in discipline, attendance, student morale, and scholarship.

Public School 63 in Indianapolis started using the Character Education Curriculum in 1970. In April 1971 Beatrice M. Bowles, principal of Public School 63, wrote the following letter to the American Institute for Character Education:

In August, 1970, I was invited to attend a session of the Character Education Workshop. The speakers were dynamic, the materials excellent, and the group stimulating. I decided at that time the Character Education Project should prove of great value at School 63.

I was appointed principal at School 63 for the school year 1970-71. On viewing the building during the months of June and July, I was very much dismayed. Many, many windows had been broken, and the glass had been replaced with masonite. The building resembled a school in a riot area. I asked that the masonite be replaced with glass, and was informed that it would be impossible as $3,500 worth of glass had been broken from September, 1969, through June, 1970. The school image in the community was very poor—"the school had gone to the dogs." When school opened, most of the pupils were rude, discourteous, and insolent to members of the faculty. The school had 99 percent black pupils and 75 percent white faculty. The children had no school pride, very poor self-image, and were most disgruntled because they had to attend "that old school."

At our first faculty meeting, Mrs. Jean English, a member of the Character Education Workshop, presented the Character Education materials. All of the staff were favorably impressed, and it was the consensus that the materials would be used at all grade levels.

Since September, 1970, there has been less than one hundred dollars' worth of glass breakage, and this has been accidental. Student attitude has greatly improved, and at the suggestion of the students, a student council was organized and is functioning. The students are now respectful and cooperative with the teachers, and there is the feeling of one for all and all for one. The building is much cleaner, and consultants, parents, fire inspectors, and others entering the building have made many complimentary remarks on the many improvements.

School 63 is well on the way to becoming the very fine educational institution for which it was intended. We attribute this remarkable change to Mrs. English, our Character Education chairman, and the use of the Character Education Project materials provided by your staff.

The above letter was written in 1971. But what happened at Wendell Phillips Public School 63 during the next five years is even more impressive. In 1976 Mrs. Bowles wrote a follow-up on the character education program:

The Character Education Program has been in continuous use at Wendell Phillips Public School 63 since September, 1970. Mrs. Jean English still serves as our Character Education chairperson, and the success of the program is indisputable. There is little teacher turnover at School 63, but the new teachers are given the needed training for teaching Character Education by Mrs. English.

The Character Education materials are interesting, stimulating, inspiring, and thought-provoking. The kindergarten children are delighted with the animal portrayal of values and participate wholeheartedly in the class discussions. The inclusion of many nationalities of children has also added much to acceptability of the materials. After six years of usage, the pupils, parents, and teachers are still enthusiastic about and enthralled with the program. I often plan classroom visitations at the time when Character Education materials are presented because I too continue to enjoy them. The materials are often correlated with Language Arts, Social Studies, and Art. Many writing exercises have been the spontaneous results of Character Education materials.

The use of Character Education materials has greatly enhanced the lives of pupils, parents, and teachers at School 63. Yearly, the last week in September or the first week in October, each teacher has a room meeting with pupils and parents. The curriculum, including Character Education, to be covered by June of the following year is presented, and the parents become involved. They have always been very supportive and excited about the Character Education materials. As a result of this meeting, we have three-way involvement: parent-pupil-teacher. All have greatly benefited as manifested in improved relationships between parent-child, parent-parent, and parent-teacher. Our PTA is active and progressing.

Discipline and vandalism are no problems at School 63. Our children are well behaved, courteous, and with few exceptions, achieving at maximum potential. Our parents are concerned and cooperative. Visitors and workmen coming into the school often remark about the wonderful learning atmosphere prevalent in the building—something you can feel.

In the Character Education Program at Wendell Phillips School 63 we stress responsibility, helpfulness, honesty, generosity, tolerance, truthfulness, and other values. There is a noticeable improvement in the attitudes, behavior, and achievement of our children, now sixth graders, who have been in the program the entire six school years. School attendance is compulsory; church attendance is not, so to my staff and me Character Education is a must *in our school.*[12]

Valley Vista Elementary School in Chula Vista, California, started using the Character Education Curriculum in 1971. "Disciplinary problems almost disappeared," Mike Martin, one of the Valley Vista teachers, told a group of school administrators.

Martin was one of three Chula Vista teachers who attended a Character Education Workshop presented by the American Institute for Character Education. The three teachers had just been transferred to Valley Vista, a new elementary school in a high-income residential area.

Only about half of the students, however, came from nearby homes. The others were bused in from a very low-income neighborhood in National City. Disciplinary problems were severe, and within a short time many of the shrubs and trees at Valley Vista School had been destroyed. There were many complaints from neighboring homes because of litter, vandalism, and trampled flower gardens.

Mike Martin and his associates began using the Character Education materials. Within a few weeks, other teachers became interested in what they were doing and Mr. Martin conducted a training session for all of the teachers at Valley Vista.

The results were remarkable. Disciplinary problems almost disappeared in the classroom, in the cafeteria, and on the school grounds. The school principal, who had been spending most of his time with disciplinary problems, found that he now had time to spend in more productive ways. Trees and shrubs on the school grounds were replaced and the students left them alone. Complaints from homes near the school were greatly reduced.

Estimated costs of vandalism for a period of thirty-six months after the Character Education program was instituted were compared with previous costs, and figures showed that vandalism had been reduced to about one-thirteenth of the previous cost.

Martin said that it took almost two years to achieve full benefits from the program. This, he explained, was because much of the vandalism at the school was caused by junior high school students who were graduates from Valley Vista. These previous students, who still held resentments about the school, were the ones who returned and caused much of the damage. The use of systematic character instruction in every classroom greatly reduced student resentment and consequently vandalism.[13]

Many other schools have reported similar success stories as a result of using the Character Education Curriculum, and these reports include schools with multiracial populations and representing various economic levels. Here are a few examples:

We were concerned with school break-ins, vandalism, graffiti and especially pupil relationships to one another; since adopting the program practically all of these problems have disappeared.

New Richmond, Wisconsin[14]

We're impressed with the program for two reasons— improved attendance and discipline. We have the statistics which will show that the ADA has increased over the last year and a half from 85 percent to an average of 95 percent ADA. We have a reduction of 40 percent or more of the discipline problems referred to the principal's office for action.

John J. Pershing Elementary School San Antonio, Texas[15]

The Character Education Program has been substantially successful in our school in the development of student values, in positively influencing pupil attitudes and in improving pupil social relationships in general. . . . Equally significant is the fact Character Education appears to have assisted in improving the level of achievement of pupils involved.[16]

Fifty-Ninth Street Elementary School Los Angeles, California[16]

We are spending less time counseling individual students, discipline referrals have been drastically decreased, attendance vastly improved, vandalism is

51

virtually nonexistent, and students demonstrate real school spirit.

> Columbia Elementary School
> Champaign, Illinois[17]

I've found that the behavior of most of the children improved tremendously. Children like to relate their experiences with others. They have an opportunity to really look at themselves as others see them.

> Second-Grade Teacher
> Shenandoah Elementary
> Dade County, Florida[18]

THE MODESTO STORY

What can happen when an entire school district emphasizes responsible behavior is remarkably demonstrated by Modesto City schools in California.

In addition to reading, writing, and arithmetic, Modesto students learn the fourth *R*—responsibility.

Early in 1981 the Modesto story received national coverage by NBC as part of its week-long series "Education in America." Christopher Michon, who produced the series segment on basic education, said Modesto was selected after he talked to more than a hundred educators. "I was trying to find one school system which has gone completely back to the basics . . . and Modesto's name kept coming up," Michon said.

Modesto's Fourth R program began in 1976. James C. Enochs, assistant superintendent for curriculum and instruction, was the principal architect. Superintendent Bert C. Corona gave Dr. Enochs the green light and the necessary top-level support.

In 1979 Phi Delta Kappa Educational Foundation published a pamphlet titled "The Restoration of Standards: The Modesto Plan" by James Enochs. It described the program in full detail. With remarkable candor, Enochs wrote:

It is time to admit it: In the last dozen years, educators have made a mess of things. The evidence against us is overwhelming.˙ When children are safer on the streets than in their schools, when we are spending more on vandalism than on textbooks, and when we are clothing functional illiterates in caps and gowns, the time has come to start plea-bargaining. We are guilty.

To be sure, we have had our share of accomplices: critics... the media... pop psychologists... social engineers.... There is little we can offer in our defense. After all, many of us went along. In the name of innovation and relevancy, we suspended our better judgment.... The result was an egalitarianism so ill conceived as, in Kierkegaard's phrase, to be "unrelieved by even the smallest eminence."... Intelligence tests were suddenly suspect because some legal-aid lawyers charged they were "culturally biased." Ability grouping became known as undemocratic stereotyping. Grading was referred to as an arbitrary system of rewards and punishments meted out by authoritarian teachers....

In sorting through the professional literature of the time, one finds elaborate, jargon-filled justifications for all of this. The pages are peppered with "scholarly" footnotes calling to witness the gurus of the day....

But there was an even more appealing element in their siren call, a kind of hidden melody that we could never publicly acknowledge: It was all simply easier that way. If there were no standardized benchmarks against which to be measured, there was no accountability. The tough, time-consuming process of monitoring— teachers monitoring students, principals monitoring teachers, superintendents monitoring principals—was lifted from our shoulders....

I choose to think we had best be about the work of restoring standards—and our credibility.[19]

Modesto schools used the 1976 Gallup poll on education (there has been little change in more recent polls) as a starting point:

- 84 percent of those with children in school favored instruction in morals and moral behavior;
- 55 percent would send their children to schools with strict discipline codes and strong emphasis on the three *R*s;
- 54 percent didn't think students were required to work hard enough;
- 96 percent favored high school graduation requirements that demand that a student be able to read well enough to follow an instruction manual, write a letter of application using correct grammar and spelling, and know enough arithmetic to be able to figure out such problems as the total square feet in a room.

This was followed by a statement of principles—a straightforward redefinition of what Modesto administrators believed in and stood for:

1. It is essential that a public institution clearly define itself; to say unequivocally what it believes in and stands for.
2. The development of responsible adults is a task requiring community commitment. It cannot be left solely to the public schools.
3. The principal tasks of the public schools cannot be achieved if a disproportionate amount of time and resources must be given to maintaining order. Public schools are not obliged to serve students who, through persistent and serious acts, disrupt school and violate the rights of others.
4. Parents must consistently support the proposition that students have responsibilities as well as rights, and schools have an obligation to insist upon both.
5. High performance takes place in a framework of expectations.
6. The full responsibility for learning cannot be transferred from the student to the teacher.
7. There is nothing inherently undemocratic in requiring students to do things that are demonstrably beneficial to them.

8. In order for a program to succeed, it must be kept in place for a reasonable period of time and be assured of continued support, despite periodic criticism and the lure of faddishness.[20]

The full program developed from this set of principles was called *Academic Expectations and the Fourth R: Responsibility*. It included the following:

Basic Skills Competency

Minimum competencies in math, reading, and writing were established for each grade level. The competency standards were written as specific skills or knowledge and widely publicized. Unless students could demonstrate these minimum skills, they could not graduate to a higher grade.

Remediation and Retention

Promotion is now determined solely on the basis of attainment of the minimum competencies in reading and arithmetic. (At present, students are not retained if they fail only the written competency.) A student may not be retained more than twice in grades K through 8. Junior high school students who have already been retained twice and are still below competency levels are placed into special remedial classes.

A Specialized High School Graduation Plan

Upon entering high school, students, with the approval of their parents, are required to select one of three curriculum plans: academic, vocational, or general. Each plan carries with it a set of special course requirements beyond the general education courses required of all students.

During the junior year all students are required to take a battery of competency tests in the applied general education areas required of all students regardless of their choice of graduation plans. If a student fails in any area, he is required, following appropriate remediation, to retake the test in his senior year. Exams in all five areas must be passed before graduation. No student is granted a diploma without accumulating a specific number of units, completing one of the graduation plans, and passing all competency tests.

Written Student Conduct Codes

Written student conduct codes setting forth student rights, responsibilities, and specific infractions and their consequences have been developed for grades K through 6 and 7 through 12. The codes are written in specific terms. Common forms of misconduct are listed and clearly defined. The consequences of a first infraction and repeated infractions are spelled out. The conduct-code handbooks are distributed to every student in the district and include a verification of receipt to be signed by the parents and returned to the school. The county code for grades 7 through 12 includes a provision for evaluating student in-class citizenship.

Character Education Curriculum

Every elementary school teacher (K through 6) uses the Character Education Curriculum developed by the American Institute for Character Education.

"The program," states Dr. Enochs, "is simply predicated on the belief that there are still some values upon which all reasonable people can agree. Any fairminded person who took the time to examine the materials, the objectives, and the manner of presentation would laugh at the charge of indoctrination."[21]

A Community Consortium for Dealing with Serious Youth Problems

This program component is administered by a standing committee of key administrators from the schools, probation department, mental-health agency, welfare department, police department, juvenile courts, and other agencies working with the young. The committee's role is to provide a forum for airing present concerns, defining responsibilities, and exploring areas of greater cooperation. The goal is to prevent children from falling into the cracks between a confusing myriad of agencies.

56

The results of the Fourth R program are most impressive. There was marked improvement in scholarship, with test scores in reading, writing, and arithmetic jumping from about 45 percent of state average to 60 or 80 percent. Attendance in 1979 was 18,500 student days better than before, saving the district $170,072, and vandalism was held to a three-year increase of 6.9 percent at a time when other California school districts were reporting a 20 to 25 percent increase in vandalism *each year.*

Tables 1a, 1b, and 1c give some of the statistics for the approximately nineteen thousand students enrolled in Modesto City schools. As to the Character Education Curriculum, Dr. Enochs states: "While it is impossible to single out which of several program elements is responsible for our steady improvement, I want you to know that Character Education is a critically important element. It is now taught on a regular basis in all of our elementary schools."[22]

IS IT EVER TOO LATE?

The preceding examples of successful character-building programs represent only a portion of the available case histories at the elementary school level.

The authors did not find nearly as many examples of systematic character education for older students. Most people tend to believe that character is formed at an early age, and once formed, does not change. Sigmund Freud's theory of personality has given strong support to this point of view.

It is probably true that most people's personality, once formed, remains relatively constant, but there are many exceptions. Lee Cronbach, in his book *Educational Psychology,* disagrees with the view that character is "set like plaster" by the age of thirty. "Character," says Professor Cronbach, "begins to set almost at the time of birth. . . . But a person can acquire new understandings and attachment to new ideals throughout his life, if at his core he likes the world, feels that the world likes him, and believes in the power of his own intelligence."[23]

Although the evidence is fragmentary, it may be that when young people reach a certain age—about the time that they enter

Table 1a
ACADEMIC GAINS SINCE ADOPTION OF ACADEMIC
EXPECTATIONS AND THE FOURTH R. RESPONSIBILITY

California Assessment Program
(California Norms)

	1975–76 (Pre-4th R)	1979-80	Gain or Loss
Grade 3			
Reading	47%ile (A)*	68%ile (A)	+21%
Written language	Not tested	66%ile (A)	
Mathematics	Not tested	76%ile (A)	
Grade 6			
Reading	39%ile (W)	59%ile (A)	+20%
Writing	38%ile (B)	60%ile (A)	+22%
Spelling	40%ile (B)	80%ile (A)	+40%
Mathematics	41%ile (W)	80%ile (A)	+39%
Grade 12			
Reading	47%ile (W)	73%ile (A)	+26%
Writing	46%ile (W)	62%ile (A)	+16%
Spelling	38%ile (B)	78%ile (A)	+40%
Mathematics	44%ile (W)	69%ile (A)	+25%

* Modesto scores are compared with scores of districts in California which statistically are like Modesto.

    (A)—Above comparison score band.
    (W)—Within comparison score band.
    (B)—Below comparison score band.

junior high school—the needed approach shifts from prevention to rehabilitation. Most children, in other words, reach an age where they have acquired negative attitudes and habits. After this, if their character is to be improved, they must be taught how to change negative attitudes into positive attitudes.

William Glasser, psychiatrist and author of the popular text *Reality Therapy,* insists that it is never too late to teach character. "The teaching of responsibility," he states, "is the most important task of all higher animals.... That it can be taught only to the young is not true.... Responsibility can be learned at any age."[24] His position is significantly different from that of conventional psychiatry, which, according to Dr. Glasser, "scrupulously avoids the problem, that is, whether the patient's behavior is right or wrong."[25]

Table 1b
STANDARDIZED ACHIEVEMENT TESTS
COMPREHENSIVE TEST OF BASIC SKILLS

Percent of Students Above the 50th Percentile

	1975–76 (Pre-4th R)	1979–80	Gain or Loss
Grade 3			
Reading	56%	69%	+13%
Mathematics	58%	71%	+13%
Grade 4			
Reading	50%	64%	+14%
Mathematics	48%	70%	+22%
Grade 5			
Reading	54%	63%	+ 9%
Mathematics	50%	72%	+22%
Grade 6			
Reading	52%	63%	+11%
Mathematics	50%	70%	+20%

Table 1c
COLLEGE ADMISSIONS TESTING PROGRAM (ATP)

	1975–76 (Pre-4th R)	1979–80	Gain or Loss
Scholastic Aptitude Test			
Verbal	432	450	+18 points
Mathematics	482	493	+11 points
National Mean			
Verbal		425	
Mathematics		466	

CHANGING CRIMINAL BEHAVIOR THROUGH CHARACTER EDUCATION

Dr. Glasser and his associates found that unless people judged their own behavior, they would not change. "People do not act irresponsibly because they are 'ill'; they are 'ill' because they act irresponsibly."[26] The success of Reality Therapy was

59

demonstrated at the Ventura School for Girls, a state institution that houses the most serious delinquents in California—girls from fourteen to twenty-one years of age who have committed offenses ranging from incorrigibility to first-degree murder. The girls were characterized by their lack of deep feeling for themselves or anyone else and by a common history of taking the easy irresponsible course when any choice was presented. Dr. Glasser's objective for every girl, no matter how antagonistic, was to rehabilitate her within six to eight months so that, with the assistance of a parole officer, she would stay out of further serious trouble in the community. The result of this demonstration, described in detail in *Reality Therapy,* was that the rate of success, as measured by reduced recidivism, increased from about 40 percent to more than 75 percent.

EMOTIONAL MATURITY INSTRUCTION

Emotional Maturity Instruction is a remarkably successful ethical instruction program for juvenile and adult criminals. The method is the result of years of research by a Georgia attorney, Daniel MacDougald. He attributes the basic idea underlying Emotional Maturity Instruction to Dr. William James, early American psychologist, who said, "Human beings can alter their lives by altering their attitudes of mind."[27]

Our behavior, according to MacDougald, is the result of mental habits—habitual and often unrecognized attitudes, values, and goals. Delinquents, criminals, drug addicts, and alcoholics have developed unhealthy or unproductive mental habits.

The course is designed for individual or small-group instruction, preferably not more than eight or ten individuals in a group. It is taught in twelve two-hour sessions—one session each week with three additional sessions needed for psychological testing.

The teaching process is highly Socratic. Instructors are taught to ask questions which force students to think about and crystallize their goals, attitudes, and values. Students are taught the importance of setting and achieving positive personal goals.

Although the process avoids indoctrination, participants are encouraged to study and adopt basic Judeo-Christian values such as respect and consideration for others.

Emotional Maturity Instruction has been in use in Dougherty County, Georgia, since 1970.

In 1974 Luciano L'Abate, Georgia State University psychology professor, did an independent evaluation of juveniles who received Emotional Maturity Instruction. Dr. L'Abate states:

> *I examined every third folder of the Judicial Service Agency files which included a delinquent case. From this sample, three groups were formed and the analysis of each group revealed (1) Emotional Maturity Instruction is effective in reducing repeat offenses. For instance, 71 percent of the group receiving Emotional Maturity Instruction was reported as not repeating delinquency for the period under investigation from 1970 to the present. (2) The testing program revealed an ability beyond chance to predict that taking Emotional Maturity Instruction changes the testing profiles of the persons completing the program. These changes were in the direction of noncriminality or normality.*[28]

In 1977 John Fisher, a psychology-criminal justice intern at Albany Junior College, made still another attempt to evaluate the effectiveness of Emotional Maturity Instruction. He examined the juvenile court files of 3,762 juveniles for the period from July 1, 1970, to June 30, 1976. He found that for 840 juvenile criminals who received Emotional Maturity Instruction, the failure rate was 22.9 percent. Juvenile criminals who did not receive Emotional Maturity Instruction during the test period had a failure rate of 66 percent.[29]

A still more recent study of Emotional Maturity Instruction in Dougherty County was made by Albany police detective Carl Schmidt. In the beginning, when he decided to evaluate the program for his Ph.D. in criminology, Schmidt was convinced that the program was ineffective. Previous evaluations, he wrote, varied from highly positive to very negative.

Detective Schmidt studied all felons placed on probation by the Superior Court of Dougherty County, Georgia, from

January 1, 1969, through December 31, 1977. During this period 814 criminals on probation received Emotional Maturity Instruction. This group was compared with 753 criminals, also on probation, who did not receive the program.

Recidivism (failure), for the purpose of this study, was defined as any further meaningful arrest or probation warrant, including "driving under the influence" but excluding other traffic violations. A meaningful arrest was defined as one leading to a negative determination at a probation revocation hearing.

"The improvement and success ratios between the control group and the experimental group, by the simple addition of EMI," writes Detective Schmidt, "is utterly astonishing. It is astonishing that adding Emotional Maturity Instruction to the probation process renders it so effective.... This researcher has checked, rechecked, and checked the facts again. The facts are as stated. The assessment criteria for both groups is the same. The 'wild' claims of Emotional Maturity Instruction system users that they can reduce recidivism to 35 percent or less are actually conservative claims."[30]

The statistics on which Schmidt based his conclusions are as follows: for the control group for 1969 through 1977, there were 720 recidivists out of the 753. That is a 96 percent failure rate. For the 814 parolees who received Emotional Maturity Instruction, there were 187 recidivists—a failure rate of 23 percent.

ACHIEVEMENT SKILLS

Achievement Skills is the title of a series of instructional workbooks developed by the Thomas Jefferson Research Center for use in an educational setting. The program is somewhat similar to Emotional Maturity Instruction but is designed as a series of workbooks—one for each grade level for seven through twelve and an additional workbook for college/adult use.

The program is so new that there has not been an opportunity to conduct an adequate evaluation of the program's effectiveness.

Although not conclusive, a recent test of the eighth-grade level is most encouraging. In May 1981 Jerry Hill, chief probation officer in San Bernardino, California, began using the

Achievement Skills program in a twenty-bed residential center for delinquent males, sixteen and a half to eighteen years of age. These young criminals had all committed multiple or serious offenses and had failed on probation and prior court placements.

Ten juveniles entered the forty-five-hour program, meeting for one hour three times each week. Seven of this group graduated.

Geri Olin, staff psychologist, sought to determine whether the Achievement Skills program was effective in improving the attitudes, values, and self-image of these young delinquents. Tennessee Self-Concept Scale pretest scores were compared with posttest scores of the seven juveniles who completed the program. Analysis of the test data established that there was improvement on the moral-ethical self-image at the .10 level of significance for 90 percent of those completing Achievement Skills.

To establish that this improvement was not influenced by other variables, a comparison group of seven juveniles also received the Tennessee Self-Concept Scale Test. There was no significant change between pretest and posttest scores for this group.

Although the results of this pilot project were not conclusive because of the small number of juveniles involved, Dr. Olin felt that the results were extremely encouraging and recommended a larger research project.

Judge Douglas McDaniel, who was influential in introducing the program in San Bernardino, said that in all of his years of experience as a judge, he had never seen such dramatic changes in the attitudes of a group of juvenile delinquents.[31]

CHARACTER EDUCATION IS FEASIBLE

Is systematic character education in public schools feasible? The answer for elementary schools is an unequivocal yes. For older students, although the evidence is not as compelling, the authors are thoroughly convinced that once again the answer is yes.

Chapter 5

THE SEPARATION OF CHURCH AND STATE

Without a moral and spiritual awakening there is no hope for us.

Dwight D. Eisenhower

One of the major objections to the idea that public schools should place greater emphasis on character development is the conviction that ethical principles cannot, or at least should not, be taught separately from religion.

Several years ago, the Thomas Jefferson Research Center was interviewing candidates to write copy for one of the Center's character-building programs.

The job was offered to the applicant who seemed best qualified, but he declined, stating that he felt the assignment was in conflict with his religious convictions as a Roman Catholic.

Several weeks later he called and said that he had discussed this conflict with several of his former professors at Loyola University in Los Angeles. They had informed him that the Roman Catholic church had no objection to character education separate from religion, provided that the principles taught were compatible. They pointed out that Confucianism was a moral philosophy rather than a religion, and that it was perfectly proper for an individual to be both Catholic and Confucian.

The Loyola professors went on to tell the writer that just after the end of World War II, General Chiang Kai-shek asked some

Catholic scholars to help develop a program to teach moral principles in Chinese schools. He wanted a program that was compatible with all of the various religions represented in China. The Catholic scholars assured him that it was quite feasible to develop an ethical education program based on reason and logic rather than on divine revelation. Unfortunately, this effort was cut short by the communist takeover in China.

Many Americans believe that the Supreme Court has ruled against ethical instruction in public schools. This is not true. The First Amendment to the U.S. Constitution states, "Congress shall make no law respecting an establishment of religion, or prohibiting the free exercise thereof."

Much of the misunderstanding of the Supreme Court's position stems from the 1963 *Abington School District* v. *Schempp* decision by the Court. This decision did not forbid teaching moral or spiritual values or even teaching *about* the Bible. What was found unconstitutional under the "establishment of religion" clause was a Baltimore School Board statute requiring reading from the Bible without comment at the opening of each school day and the recitation of the Lord's Prayer by the students in unison. The Court decided eight to one that such school exercises violate the First Amendment.

William J. Brennan, Jr., one of the concurring judges, wrote:

> *The holding of the Court today plainly does not foreclose teaching about the Holy Scriptures or about the differences between religious sects in classes of literature or history. Indeed, whether or not the Bible is involved, it would be impossible to teach meaningfully many subjects in the social sciences or the humanities without some mention of religion. To what extent, and at what points in the curriculum religious material should be cited, are matters which the courts ought to entrust very largely to the experienced officials who superintend our nation's public schools. They are experts in such matters, and we are not.*[1]

The following statement of policy and position on religion in public education was jointly adopted by the Synagogue Council of America and the National Community Relations Advisory

Council and represents a position designed to meet Supreme Court standards:

> *Insofar as the teaching of spiritual values may be understood to signify religious teaching, this must remain, as it has been, the responsibility of the home, the church, and the synagogue. Insofar as it is understood to signify the teaching of morality, ethics, and good citizenship, a deep commitment to such values has been successfully inculcated by our public schools in successive generations of Americans. The public schools must continue to share responsibility for fostering our commitment to these moral values, without presenting or teaching any sectarian or theological sources or sanctions for such values.[2]*

In *Pierce* v. *Society of Sisters,* the U.S. Supreme Court considered the rights and responsibilities of parents and schools in educating children. The Court found that parents had the right to "direct the upbringing and education of children under their control." This in effect ensured the right of parents to send their children to the school of their choice.

In addition to affirming the right of parents to select the school of their choice, however, the Court went on to state:

> *No question is raised concerning the power of the state reasonably to regulate all schools, to inspect, supervise and examine them, their teachers and pupils, to require that all children of proper age attend some school, that teachers shall be of good moral character and patriotic disposition,* that certain studies plainly essential to good citizenship must be taught, *and that nothing be taught which is manifestly inimical to the public welfare.[3] [Emphasis added]*

Interestingly, the famous Northwest Ordinance, enacted in 1787, was approved by the same Congress that wrote and approved the U.S. Constitution, and it was much the same group that passed the First Amendment to the Constitution four years later.

The Northwest Ordinance stated: "Religion, morality, and knowledge being necessary to good government and the happiness of mankind, schools and the means of education shall forever be encouraged."[4]

Although the Constitution itself does not refer to ethical instruction, there are many references to its importance by the architects of the Constitution. Thomas Jefferson said, "Virtue is not hereditary"; and, "I know of no safe repository for the ultimate powers of society but the people themselves; and if we think them not enlightened enough to exercise their control with a wholesome direction, the remedy is not to take it from them, but to increase their discretion by education."[5]

Madison said, "To suppose that any form of government will secure liberty or happiness without any virtue in the people, is a chimerical idea."[6]

"I thank God," said Samuel Adams, "that I have lived to see my country independent and free. She may enjoy her independence and freedom if she will. It depends on her virtue."[7]

Franklin was equally vehement. "Only a virtuous people are capable of freedom. As nations become corrupt and vicious, they have more need of masters. . . . Nothing is of more importance for the public weal, than to form and train up youth in wisdom and virtue."[8]

Several years ago the Maryland General Assembly passed a resolution instructing the governor to appoint a commission to "identify and assess ongoing programs in morals and value education in the schools of Maryland, if any, and to make recommendations toward the implementation of these programs into the curriculum."[9]

The new commission asked the state attorney general to give it a legal opinion on whether there are any legal impediments to the teaching of ethical values in public schools. In July 1979 the commission received a seven-page opinion from Attorney General Stephen H. Sachs, who stated in part:

We have concluded that the fact that ethical values are taught in the public school system does not, standing alone, violate the Establishment and Free Exercise Clauses of the First Amendment of the United States Constitution or any privacy rights arising under the

First Amendment.... Religion certainly cannot be construed to envelop an educational program that attempts merely to impart basic ethical and moral values to the children of this society. On this point, the District Court in Malnak v. Yogi *stated:*

"Similarly, principles which society at large finds beneficial and useful are not religious in nature merely because similar principles are common to the dogmas of many religious sects. For example, a public school could teach its students that it is wrong to steal or murder without violating the establishment clause. The public school could not teach its students to refrain from stealing because God has proscribed it. The principle is not necessarily religious, but becomes religious if taught as a divine law. 440 F. Supp. at 1316–17, n. 20.3"

Consequently, the fact that an educational program teaches moral and ethical views that have their roots in the Judeo-Christian heritage would not, of itself, make such activity religious in nature.... Values education serves the legitimate secular purpose of preparing individuals to be self-reliant and self-sufficient participants in society.... However, it is important to point out that although, in theory, the teaching of values in the public school system is not constitutionally deficient, certain specific subjects and methodologies taught or employed in the name of "values education" could, in fact, violate the religion clauses or the privacy rights of a student....

In conclusion, it is our belief that values education may be included in Maryland's curriculum for its public schools without infringing on any First Amendment rights. Of course, such programs must steer a neutral course in the religious sphere and maintain the firm wall that separates our religious and secular lives. Also, such courses must preserve the classroom as a true "market place of ideas" and avoid a "religion of secularism" or the indoctrination of one-sided views.[10]

THERE MUST BE A CLEAR SEPARATION

There should be no doubt that the inclusion of religious indoctrination with the teaching of character education in the public schools is not only illegal but unethical as well. In establishing a program systematically to teach schoolchildren the values of honesty, integrity, respect for law, and the other enduring cross-cultural and universal values, there is always the possibility that someone, somewhere, will breach the gap that separates the teaching of religion from the teaching of character.

The person who chooses to indoctrinate students, however, will probably find ways to carry on this pursuit no matter whether the curriculum is one of character education, social studies, or some other curricular offering.

That a few educators violate the principle of separation of church and state should not be cause for abandoning the teaching of ethical values. Daniel Callahan and Sissela Bok, in their study of the teaching of ethics at the university level, state:

It would be wholly out of place for university teachers to indoctrinate students with their own moral values or theories, and in particular to do so in a way that precludes exposure to other moral perspectives. But to let anxiety over the possibility of indoctrination dictate an omission of courses in ethics strikes us as equally odd. While there is always such a risk in higher education—in economics, politics, or law, for example—it is no greater in courses on ethics. Teaching approaches that are reprehensible in other fields are no less so in ethics courses. If one believes, as we do, that enabling students to reach their own moral judgments is an important goal of ethics teaching, then the chances of indoctrination are reduced from the start. Faculty should be free to express their viewpoints; failure to do so could represent a special kind of moral bankruptcy. But they have a fundamental obligation to make certain students understand that there are different moral viewpoints—and to help them develop

70

the skills necessary to analyze the teacher's moral values as well as other moral positions."

A careful definition of what values will be included in a character education program can lessen the anxiety and bring a degree of understanding and perhaps resolution to the debate concerning the implementation of character education. "Our task," says Secretary of Education Terrel H. Bell, "is to consider ways of deliberately, systematically, and effectively carrying out moral education in the schools—and to do this in a way that violates none of the ethnic, racial, or religious differences that characterize our country's children."[12]

ETHICAL INSTRUCTION IS REQUIRED IN SOME STATES

In the preceding pages we have described legal decisions to show that character education in public schools is legal. The fact is, it is not only legal, but required by law in several states. For example, section 44806 of the California Education Code reads:

Training of Pupils in Morality and Citizenship

Each teacher shall endeavor to impress upon the minds of the pupils the principles of morality, truth, justice, patriotism, and a true comprehension of the rights, duties, and dignity of American citizenship, including kindness toward domestic pets and the humane treatment of living creatures, to teach them to avoid idleness, profanity, and falsehood, and to instruct them in manners and morals and principles of a free government.[13]

In Michigan the State Board of Education adopted a resolution (March 13, 1968) that stated in part:

RESOLVED, that the State Board of Education urges educators in the schools of Michigan to continue to improve their efforts to foster thoughtful and critical

71

examination of moral values by students and to provide them with the opportunity to practice and demonstrate these values both in the classroom and in extracurricular activities of school, and in their everyday life, so that each student can improve the quality of his own life and of society as a whole. Included in the values which should be particularly developed are self-respect, respect for others, respect for the law, and good citizenship.[14]

Following that action, the Michigan State Board of Education adopted a Resolution on Moral Values and Value Systems (August 28, 1968), which states as follows:

We, the members of the State Board of Education, believe strongly—

That to function as a responsible citizen in our complex world, each individual should have available not only "the facts," but a sound set of values upon which to base his decisions; and

That each youngster should be aided in making his choice of values not only by his parents and church, but by the schools; and

That, while the public schools in a democracy must not attempt to inculcate any specific set of values, the public schools may assist the student in his understanding of the numerous value systems and their historical basis.

We are concerned—

That few, if any, schools provide information to students, formally and systematically, about the need for values and the numerous values and value systems held by individuals and groups throughout the world; and

72

That part of the reason for this lack is the absence of instructional materials which would be viewed as appropriate by the community and teachers for use in schools; and

That another part of the reason is an assumption, on the part of some school boards and educators, that some parents would object to more specific instruction about values and value systems.

We, therefore, urge—

That local boards of education and educators take leadership in their communities, in convincing parents and others that it is important for students to learn about personal value systems and critically evaluate these and other religious and ethical systems which have an impact on civilizations and institutions... [15]

Michigan and California are not alone in stressing the need for ethical instruction through the public school system. For example, the North Dakota State Code of Education says:

15-38-10. MORAL INSTRUCTION. Moral instruction tending to impress upon the minds of pupils the importance of truthfulness, temperance, purity, public spirit, patriotism, international peace, respect for honest labor, obedience to parents, and deference to old age, shall be given by each teacher in the public schools. [16]

In February 1981 the legislature of Virginia passed into law the following resolutions:

WHEREAS, Virginians are in substantial agreement regarding a number of ethical qualities judged necessary to civilized society, to democratic self-government, and to the prospering of the body politic; and

73

WHEREAS, the Virginia Constitution, in language derived from George Mason, identifies among such ethical qualities "justice, moderation, temperance, frugality, and virtue" as qualities without which "no free government, nor the blessings of liberty, can be preserved to any people"; and

WHEREAS, such ethical values as justice, temperance, virtue, honesty, industry, fairness, responsibility, loyalty, love of country, concern for others, and respect for the dignity, worth, rights, and freedoms of all persons, though these qualities are espoused by the Judaic and Christian traditions, are moral values upon which substantial consensus exists also among those who may not share either religious faith; and

WHEREAS, There is therefore no establishment of religion, nor any abridgment of the free exercise of religion, when through such consensus ethical values are fostered in public schools, or when the Virginia Constitution declares them to be duties, as when it affirms that it is "the mutual duty of all" to practice "forebearance, love, and charity toward each other"; and

WHEREAS, the Code of Virginia, since 1928, has included the provision that "the entire scheme of instruction in the public schools shall emphasize moral education"...; and

WHEREAS, the Preamble to the 1980-82 Standards of Quality for the school divisions in the Commonwealth, consistent with the Preambles to earlier Standards, declares that one of the goals of public education in Virginia is to aid each pupil to "develop ethical standards of behavior and participate in society as a responsible family member and citizen"; and

WHEREAS, approximately 80 percent of the public and 85 percent of parents of public school children favor instruction in the public schools which "would deal with morals and moral behavior," according to Gallup polls in both 1975 and 1980; and...

WHEREAS, the General Assembly is charged by the Virginia Constitution to "seek to ensure that an educational program of high quality is established and continually maintained" in the Commonwealth (Article VIII, Section 1), and the quality of such education in the public schools, reposing as it does upon the support it receives from the taxpaying citizenry, may be adversely affected by lack of information or misunderstandings among those citizens regarding the role the public schools play, and should play, in our society; now, therefore, be it

RESOLVED by the House of Delegates, the Senate concurring, That the appreciative attention of the citizenry is called to the Virginia public schools' historic emphasis, consistent with the Constitution, Code of Virginia, and Standards of Educational Quality of Virginia, on the education of Young Virginians for ethical conduct; and, be it

RESOLVED FURTHER, That efforts to make this ethics education emphasis better known and more adequately understood are encouraged, to the end that the public schools of this Commonwealth may enjoy the full measure of confidence and support which they deserve.[17]

The above resolution by the Virginia legislature provides an excellent summary of the authors' thesis—that public schools can and should systematically teach ethical values.

75

Chapter 6

HISTORICAL PERSPECTIVE

Civilization is the victory of persuasion over force.

Plato

Since ancient times, wise men have known the crucial importance of ethics and ethical instruction for individuals and society. Aristotle, for example, said, "All who have meditated on the art of governing mankind have been convinced that the fate of empires depends upon the education of youth."
Philosophy professor Andrew Oldenquist says:

> *If we were anthropologists observing members of a tribe, it would be the most natural thing in the world to expect them to teach their morality and culture to their children and, moreover, to think that they had a perfect right to do so on the ground that cultural integrity and perpetuation depend on it.*
>
> *Indeed, if we found that they had ceased to teach, through ritual and other organized means, the moral and other values of their culture, we would take them to be on the way to cultural suicide.[1]*

The information that follows is from an article by Frederick A. Manchester titled "Moral Education—and History."*

---

* In *The Freeman*, July 1968 (copyright ©1968, Foundation for Economic Education). Dr. Manchester is former professor of history, University of Wisconsin.

Dr. Norman Vincent Peale has recently been quoted as saying that "we are living in probably the most undisciplined age in history."[2] Well, if this age is indeed liable to so serious a charge, it should be of interest to know whether the past owed its differing condition to accident or whether this may have been related to specific measures which it has taken. What, in this connection, have other ages done? I suggest that we direct our attention to a few examples of past practice.

First, what about primitive cultures? At adolescence boys are given "moral instruction, including tribal usage relating to obedience, courage, truth, hospitality, sexual relationships, reticence and perseverance."[3] "Sometimes long periods of silence are imposed upon novices in connection with the puberal ceremonies of most primitive people.... Australian boys go alone into the bush, and are required to maintain silence for long periods. African lads are required to remain silent and immobile for long periods. Such practices test a boy's obedience and self-control, and render teachings associated with them especially impressive."[4]

As to education in ancient Egypt, we are told that morals were its "central feature.... Civilization demanded the evolution and enrichment of moral life. To this end the Egyptians sought to train and instruct their young in the art of virtuous living. Their method of moral cultivation was a great advance beyond the simple training of primitive society.... The sage old vizier, Ptah-hotep, in the 27th century B.C. wrote, 'Precious to a man is the virtue of his son, and good character is a thing remembered.' This is said to be the first recorded use of the word 'character' in literature.... The Egyptian use of the word character signified 'to shape, to form, or build.'"[5]

In ancient India, a boy belonging to any one of the three upper of the four castes "had to leave his father's house and go to the house of his would-be teacher and live with him until he was twenty-five, when he would have become master of all the branches of learning. The life spent in the professor's house is called the life of Brahmacharya. *This was exactly the opposite of what we call a comfortable and luxurious life. However rich his parents might be, a new student would be treated equally with his compeers. . . . The celibate students of the classical days were trained to be hardy and robust and were not only learned in the lore of the day but were also sober and thoughtful. . . . Devotion to duty and spiritual exercises practiced long in the preceptor's family made them loving, friendly, broad-minded, truthful and happy.*"[6]

Of education in ancient Greece, we can catch a glimpse in the following sentences from Plato's Protagoras: *"Education and admonition commence in the first years of childhood and last to the very end of life. Mother and nurse and father and tutor are quarreling about the improvement of the child as soon as ever he is able to understand them: he cannot say or do anything without their setting forth to him that this is just and that is unjust; this is honorable, that is dishonorable; this is holy, that is unholy; do this and abstain from that. And if he obeys, well and good; if not, he is straightened by threats and blows, like a piece of warped wood. At a later stage they send him to teachers, and enjoin them to see to his manners even more than to his reading and music. . . . And when the boy has learned his letters and is beginning to understand what is written, as before he understood only what was spoken, they put into his hands the work of great poets, which he reads at school; in these are contained many admonitions, and many tales, and praises, and encomia of ancient famous men, which he is required to learn by heart, in order that he may imitate or emulate them and desire to become like them.*"[7]

In ancient China, we are told, "The most important thing that all children were taught, was the relation between themselves and other people. . . . "8 Confucius (551–479 B.C.) was, as everyone knows, the teacher par excellence of his nation, the revered transmitter of the moral wisdom of his people accumulated through untold centuries. As early as the reign of Wu Ti (140–87 B.C.) examinations based on Confucian classics were employed as the means of selecting state officials, and subsequently this system has been characteristic of China—at least from and including the Tang Dynasty until the twentieth century.

From the Old World, I now turn for a moment to the New, specifically to Mexico. We are told that here, at the time of the Spanish conquest—"From a very early age the training of the child was very strict. . . . With such strict training it is not strange that the Spanish were astonished at the high moral tone of the natives and their reluctance to tell a lie. Unfortunately, contact between the two civilizations soon led to a rapid moral degeneration of the native code.

"Boys of what might be termed the middle class . . . were handed over to special priests for education at about the age of six, or even earlier. They were lodged in special boys' houses in an organization which might be compared to a modern boarding school, save that the discipline in the Mexican schools was much stricter. . . . Education included a very strict moral training. . . .

"Girls of the nobility and middle classes were prepared for married life by instruction in girls' schools patterned after those of the boys. They entered these at about the age of five."9

I come now, very briefly, to the post-classical period in the Occident—with special reference to America. "In the progress of western education, Christianity has

80

been the supreme influence. It is impossible to understand the institutions and culture of Occidental civilization during the past two thousand years without this new ethical force.... "[10]

"Our earliest American colleges were founded on the model of those of British universities: and here, as there, their avowed design, at the time of their foundation was not merely to raise up a class of learned men, but specifically to raise up a class of learned men for the Christian ministry.... This was the system which time had honored at Oxford and Cambridge, and which time continued to honor on this continent with slight modifications down nearly to the close of the 18th century."[11]

"The old education," said Irving Babbitt in 1924, referring to the early American colleges, "was, in intention at least, a training for wisdom and character."[12]

So much for our American colleges; now the schools. "The most prominent characteristic of all the early colonial schooling was the predominance of the religious purpose in instruction. One learned to read chiefly to be able to read the Catechism and the Bible, and to know the will of the Heavenly Father. There was scarcely any other purpose in the maintenance of elementary schools."[13]

JAPANESE SCHOOLS EMPHASIZE ETHICS

Reed J. Irvine, an authority on Japanese culture, says:

Traditionally, Oriental education was concerned more with the cultivation of character than with the mastery of skills or the acquisition of useful information. The teacher was valued as a man of high character who could, by precept and example, influence the moral development of his pupils. He was supposed to be a man of learning, but he was even more revered for his character and his exemplary conduct....

The Japanese educators were influenced by the nineteenth-century English writer Samuel Smiles, whose most famous book, Self-Help, *impressively documented the traits of character that had contributed to the great achievements of outstanding statesmen, writers, scientists and artists. Smiles, in turn, had been influenced by Plutarch, whose "lives" were written to show "virtue or vice in men" and were used to mold the character of many generations of school boys.*

Mr. Irvine says that character instruction was very successful in Japan. "Prewar Japan was poor economically, but the incidence of crime and delinquency was extremely low. It is said that not a single murder was committed in Okinawa, the poorest of all the Japanese prefectures, in the fifty years preceding World War II."[14]

In 1972 Mrs. George Romney told a Washington, D.C., audience of her recent visit to Japan. She said that a group of Japanese educators told her that American educational experts who came to Japan after the World War II surrender advised them to eliminate ethical instruction from the public school curriculum. Now, she says, the Japanese educators are convinced that this was bad advice, and they are rapidly moving to reinstate character education.[15]

EARLY AMERICAN SCHOOLS

Early American children, as we have previously stated, received far more ethical instruction than children do today. "Traditionally," states Dr. Maurice Connery, dean of the UCLA School of Social Welfare, "American education at all levels has carried a clear moral mandate whether it was expressed in the instructions and evaluations given for 'citizenship' in the primary grades or the more sophisticated moral philosophy of liberal higher education. This emphasis was muted in the swing toward scientific empiricism and the ethical relativity that has dominated our ethical orientation in the last quarter century."[16]

John R. Silber, president of Boston University, and university professor of philosophy and law, provides the following information about early American education:

Long before a child went to school, from seventeenth-century to early twentieth-century America, he learned simple verities. And he learned them first, not from teachers of philosophy or ministers of the Gospel, but literally at his mother's knee through such collections as Mother Goose. In Mother Goose we find moral lessons that were thought to be far too important to await the public schools at age six. "If wishes were horses, beggars would ride." This is Mother Goose's reminder to forget about the pleasure principle. Remember the reality principle, the child was told. Don't be misled by the attraction of wishful thinking.

Recently, I read some seventeenth- and eighteenth-century schoolbooks, used to teach reading and spelling to young American children, frequently by parents who taught their children at home. These books typically had a rhyme for every letter of the alphabet, for the authors recognized the delight that children take in rhymes. The most famous of these, The New England Primer, *begins:*

A. Adam and Eve their God did grieve.

B. Life to mend this book [the Bible] attend. *(And a picture of the Bible was shown.)*

C. The cat doth play, and after, slay. *(Cats weren't just pets in the 18th and 19th centuries; they were killers; they ate mice, and children were not protected from this grisly information.)*

D. Dogs will bite a thief at night. *(This is a warning to thieves, if not to dogs.)*

F. The idle fool is whipped at school. *(And you could add the corollary: the teacher was not sent to prison.)*

J. Job felt the rod, yet blessed his God.

Q. Queens and Kings must lie in the dust. *(This is a reminder to a child who has not yet gone to school that even kings and queens are mortal.)*

T. Time cuts down the great and small. *(In case the child was slow and had missed the point in regard to kings and queens, it is mentioned again. Repetition was recognized as conducive to learning.)*

X. Xerxes the Great shared the common fate.

Now, does the child get it? That's three times. This was a primer for first reading exercises and this was the way they taught the alphabet. And I submit that by addressing the inevitability of death several times through twenty-six letters of the alphabet, it addresses the child on a far more dignified level than that adopted by the authors of the contemporary Dick and Jane: "Spot and Jane, run and play. Run, Spot, run. Catch, Jane, catch. Dick and Jane are friends." The New England Primer was written in a period before condescension of children had been accepted as a norm for professional educators.

Consider, moreover, how children were taught to write. The art of penmanship, lost some years ago in the United States, was once taught by the use of copybooks, in which beautifully handwritten sentences were presented to the child at the head of the page, and the child was expected to imitate in his own copybook the excellently written headings. And what did the copybook heading say? What were the statements at the top of the page which the child had to copy over and over again, in the process learning them by heart? Let me read from one of the most widely used copybooks of the period.

Persevere in accomplishing a complete education....

That is the heading for a child who has not yet learned how to write. The child was expected to copy it several times. Persevere in accomplishing a complete education. Persevere in accomplishing a complete education. Persevere in accomplishing a complete education. And eventually, a big word like persevere, is learned by heart, and the meaning of perseverance is learned by persevering long enough to write it twenty times. Note the important and exciting use of truly adult words. Children like to imitate their parents; they like to go around in adult clothes, big shoes, and big hats. They also like to imitate adults by using big words. The educators of this period knew the attraction and the power of language. In these copybooks words appear as treasures, language appears as a treasure house, and education as the key. I read some others:

A stitch in time saves nine.

Quarrelsome persons are always dangerous companions.

Employment prevents vice.

An idle mind is the devil's workshop.

Great men were good boys.

Justice is a common right.

Know much, display little.

Wit should never wound.

Build your hopes of fame on virtue.

Zeal for justice is worthy of praise.

These are the efforts of an earlier generation to acquaint their children with various aspects of an undiminished reality, an unreduced reality that is the fusion of facts and values, with reality that is not merely physical, but also moral and spiritual.

85

Their concern to introduce moral and spiritual content into the education of each child expressed their concern to educate children to the full dimensions of reality—to prepare them, in short, for true human existence. It was not enough merely to talk about mathematics and arithmetic. It was not enough to talk about writing, just as a form of expression, or penmanship as a form of beautiful writing. It was important to have content in the curriculum, and that content was a distillation of a high culture.[17]

EUROPEAN EDUCATION

European educators, according to Benson and Engeman, were exposed to the same intellectual ideas that persuaded American educators gradually to abandon ethical instruction. Freud, Kant, and the existentialists were all Europeans, and Dewey and other American intellectuals were read in Europe.

The influence of these ideas, however, was less in Europe than in the United States. European countries had no First Amendment restriction regarding religion, and Freud and Dewey were taken not as seriously in Europe as in America.

"Perhaps," suggests Dr. Engeman, "because the European universities educated a smaller proportion of the population, university students were better selected and less likely to accept new doctrines as enthusiastically as did Americans."[18]

It seems obvious, from the information presented in this chapter, that many past societies recognized the need to teach their young how to be virtuous. If the reader accepts Jefferson's statement that "virtue is not hereditary," then it also seems obvious that our modern society must place greater emphasis on ethical instruction if we wish to avoid the disintegration of our society.

Chapter 7

WHOSE VALUES SHOULD BE TAUGHT?

We sow a thought and reap an act;
We sow an act and reap a habit;
We sow a habit and reap a character;
We sow a character and reap a destiny.

William Makepeace Thackeray

Whose values, people frequently ask, do you propose to teach? Those who ask this question, although they may not realize it, have been influenced by ethical relativism—the idea that there are no enduring ethical values.

When the subject to be taught is chemistry, physics, or astronomy, no one asks whose chemistry? Whose physics? Whose astronomy? It is assumed that the teacher will simply present the available information to the best of his or her ability. Everyone assumes that there is an objective reality about these subjects, in spite of the fact that our understanding of the physical sciences is neither complete nor exact.

The question, whose ethics, implies that there is no objective reality about ethics and this is exactly what the ethical relativists claim.

"Such a position of normlessness," writes Professor Philip H. Phenix,

> ...*is a denial that there are really any standards of right or wrong, of better or worse, because the whole*

human endeavor appears to be meaningless and without purpose. . . . If life is essentially meaningless, there is no point in trying to promote or to improve it. An anomic theory of values is fatal to education, as it is to any sustained cultural pursuit. Unfortunately, it is a theory all too widely held, either explicitly or tacitly, and it should be recognized as an enemy of human morale and of educational effectivness.[1]

The influence of this relativistic, value-free point of view is illustrated by this statement of Dr. Lewis Mayhew in an address given when he became president of the Association of Higher Education: "Colleges are not churches, clinics nor even parents. Whether or not a student burns a draft card, participates in a civil rights march, engages in premarital sexual activity, becomes pregnant, attends church, sleeps all day or drinks all night, is not really the concern of an educational institution."[2]

The problem with this point of view is that it is not realistic and leads to increasing crime and violence and other costly manifestations of social disintegration. There *are* basic ethical principles that are necessary to social progress, and these principles must be identified and discussed and taught.

American Viewpoint, whose Good American Program was described in Chapter 4, based its program on an empirical code of ethics. The code was developed by writing to hundreds of outstanding citizens and asking their opinions. From this was developed a list of values which had been "hammered out on the anvil of practical experience." The Good American list includes such concepts as conservation, courage, personal health, honesty, initiative, perseverance, reliability, self-mastery, cooperation, courtesy, fairness, respect, tolerance, duty, independence, patriotism, responsibility, and understanding.

The American Institute for Character Education, which developed the Character Education Curriculum also described in detail in Chapter 4, based its program on a worldwide study of value systems. This study identified fifteen basic values shared by all major cultures and world religions. These values are courage, conviction, generosity, kindness, helpfulness, honesty, honor, justice, tolerance, the sound use of time and talents, freedom of choice, freedom of speech, good citizenship, the right to be an individual, and the right of equal opportunity.

This code of personal values, now taught in thousands of classrooms, has not proved to be controversial.

In California the Los Angeles city school system has developed a teacher's guide for ethical instruction that includes this introductory statement:

> *People of every culture in every age have expressed their ideals in innumerable ways. The Los Angeles Unified School District here seeks to translate into understanding and action certain concepts that are based on the heritage of the past, and describe values of our ever-evolving society: integrity, courage, responsibility, justice, reverence, love, and respect for law and order are among these concepts.*[3]

ELEMENTS OF RESPONSIBLE BEHAVIOR

The Thomas Jefferson Research Center has developed a code of behavior based on its study of outstanding leaders (see Table 2). Table 2 seeks to show that there is an optimum point for most ethical principles. Too much of a good thing, in other words, may not be good.

This list of values, when properly defined, understood, and practiced, can lead to health, happiness, and success for the individual and society.

REDISCOVERING THE AMERICAN ETHIC

America's Founding Fathers were convinced that ethical instruction was essential to maintaining the social system that they had created. Thomas Jefferson said so many times, and Franklin, Madison, Washington, and other early Americans agreed with Jefferson. Said Franklin, "Nothing is more

89

Table 2
ELEMENTS OF RESPONSIBLE BEHAVIOR

Impracticability	RESPONSIBILITY	Irresponsibility
Sophistication	WISDOM	Ignorance
Compromise	INTEGRITY	Deceit
Indulgence	LOVE	Hate
License	FREEDOM	Slavery
Sentimentality	JUSTICE	Injustice
Recklessness	COURAGE	Cowardice
Self-depreciation	HUMILITY	Arrogance
Expediency	PATIENCE	Apathy
Over achievement	INDUSTRIOUSNESS	Laziness
Miserliness	THRIFTINESS	Wastefulness
Spendthrift	GENEROSITY	Greed
Emotionalism	OBJECTIVITY	Inflexibility
Indifference	COOPERATION	Conflict
Austerity	MODERATION	Indulgence
Unrealism	OPTIMISM	Pessimism

important for the public weal than to form and train up youth in wisdom and virtue."[4]

Most Americans have been taught that the United States was founded on the Judeo-Christian ethic. This is not entirely correct. The American ethic is compatible with Judeo-Christian principles, but it includes ideas about economics, government, law, education, and ethics that were more directly derived from the Founders' study of history and philosophy.

Although their religious viewpoints differed, the Founders all believed in a purposeful, rational, God-created universe.

Thomas Paine spoke for most of the Founders when he said: "When we survey the work of creation ... we see unerring order and universal harmony reigning throughout the whole. No part contradicts another. ... God is the power of first cause, Nature is the law, and matter is the subject acted upon."[5]

This was the starting point for the American ethic—the idea that the universe was orderly and regulated by rational laws that could be discovered by the study of history, philosophy, religion, and man himself. This basic tenet was stated explicitly in the Declaration of Independence: "When in the course of human events, it becomes necessary for one people to dissolve the political bonds which have connected them with another, and to assume among the powers of the earth, the separate and equal station to which the Laws of Nature and of Nature's God entitle them... "[6]

To say that the United States was founded on the Judeo-Christian ethic alone is to ignore the fact that the principles upon which this nation was founded were considered to be universal and applicable to people of all faiths. Walter Kaufmann, Princeton professor of philosophy, has pointed out that the Founders were influenced at least as much by the Greeks and Romans as by the Jews.

Carl L. Becker, distinguished professor of history at Cornell University from 1917 to 1941, wrote:

> *Not all Americans... would have accepted the philosophy of the Declaration, just as Jefferson phrased it, without qualification, as the "common sense of the subject"; but one may say that the premises of this philosophy, the underlying preconceptions from which it was derived, were commonly taken for granted. There is a "natural order" of things in the world, cleverly and expertly designed by God for the guidance of mankind, that the "law" of this natural order may be discovered by human reason; that these laws so discovered furnished a reliable and immutable standard for testing the ideas, the conduct, and the institutions of men—these were the accepted premises, the preconceptions of most eighteenth-century thinking, not only in America, but also in England and France.[7]*

The gradual abandonment of the American ethic began more than a hundred years ago. It was then that the approach to human problems began to shift from theologians, philosophers, and historians to the behavioral scientists. Excited by scientific success in solving complex technical problems, scholars set out to use the same scientific methods to solve human problems. The practical lessons of history, philosophy, and religion were, for the most part, ignored—labeled unscientific.

The social and behavioral scientists were not the only ones who gradually abandoned the American ethic and its emphasis on ethical instruction, but they certainly played an influential role.

"If the object of education is the improvement of men," wrote Robert M. Hutchins,

> then any system of education that is without values is a contradiction in terms. A system that seeks bad values is bad. A system that denies the existence of values denies the possibility of education. Relativism, scientism, skepticism, and anti-intellectualism, the Four Horsemen of the philosophical Apocalypse, have produced that chaos in education which will end in the disintegration of the West."[8]

Now, fortunately, there is a small but growing scholarly rediscovery of the American ethic. Few of those involved would describe their ideas in this way but might think of their work as a rediscovery of ethical principles or individual responsibility or rational man.

Professors Peck and Havighurst, for example, suggest that basic ethical principles may have a scientific basis:

> It is just beginning to be conceivable that we may be able to collect some arguable facts about human nature which will, once and for all, demonstrate that the ethical principles held by the Rational Altruists are not just a nice sentiment, but a set of directions for living based on the deepest, most inexorable demands of human nature. . . . Whiting and Child make a similar observation, from the most relevant kind of cross-cultural data, "the confirmation (of our predictions) has been sufficient, we feel, to suggest strongly that there are some principles of personality development which hold true for mankind in general and not just for Western culture."[9]

The work of the late American psychologist, Dr. Abraham Maslow, is especially significant in this regard. Not only did Maslow, *as a scientist,* recognize the failure of value-free behavioral science, but he also developed a viable, alternative scientific theory—the Third Force—which is compatible with the religion-based American ethic.

"This is not an improvement of something," he wrote about his theory; "it is a real change in direction altogether. It is as if we have been going North and are now going South instead."[10]

Maslow was convinced that the methods of the physical sciences were not suitable for the study of people. He said, "Most of the psychology on this . . . value-free, value-neutral model of science . . . is certainly not false but merely trivial. . . . This model which developed from the study of objects and things has been illegitimately used for the study of human beings. It is a terrible technique. It has not worked."[11]

He suggested that the study of human beings should emphasize success and health, the study of the best specimens, rather than the study of neurotic people, rats, pigeons, and statistically average humans.

Another important feature of his approach was his insistence on the acceptance of *all* sources of knowledge about people. "It is both useful and correct," he wrote, "to consider as falling within the definition of knowledge, all 'protoknowledge' so long as its probability of being correct is greater than chance."[12] This radical (to science) idea reopens the door to the consideration of history, philosophy, and religion.

From a study of healthy human specimens, people he described as "self-actualizers"—Thomas Jefferson, Albert Einstein, Eleanor Roosevelt, Jane Addams, William James, Albert Schweitzer, Abraham Lincoln, and others—Maslow concluded that all humans shared common basic psychological needs. These basic needs are biological in origin, and either unchanging or changing so slowly that for all practical purposes they are unchanging. These needs are weak in the sense that many individuals never discover them, but also strong in that when they are insufficiently met, the result is emotional disturbance, depression, pathology.

"The ultimate disease of our time," said Maslow, "is valuelessness. . . . This state is more crucially dangerous than ever before in history."[13] His research led him to the conclusion that there were enduring ethical principles, as all major religions have claimed, but now one can study these principles using a rational, systematic approach.

Maslow, in other words, created a scientific explanation of human behavior that is compatible with the Founding Fathers' theory of natural law. But since the new theory is scientific, it can be taught in public schools and colleges where religious instruction is forbidden.

Chapter 8

HOW TO TEACH CHARACTER

In proportion, as the structure of a government gives force to public opinion, it is essential that public opinion is enlightened.

George Washington

How should schools approach the task of teaching ethical values? Perhaps the logical starting point is for teachers and administrators to become familiar with the kinds of information contained in this book. They need to be familiar with the laws in their state and county pertaining to ethical instruction. They should know the history of character instruction and the benefits that may be derived from such instruction. They need to discover what other educators are doing and what programs are available.

The California School Board Association (CSBA) created a character education task force, and in August 1982 this group issued a report titled "A Reawakening: Character Education and the Role of the School Board Member." "Ethics," the report states, "can and should be taught. Schools share this responsibility with all society.... Although parents are the first role models for children, teachers are the second. Teachers must reinforce signals that enable children to distinguish between right and wrong. Our society (and every society throughout the centuries) has established codes of ethics common to all."[1]

The task force urged California school boards to take the following steps to promote character education in the schools:

- Boards should assume responsibility for character education. Historically, public education for all in America has been justified by the need in a democratic society for literate, informed, and moral citizens.
- The electorate is accusing the schools of neglecting to teach character education. Therefore, based on historical precedent and the demands of the community that the schools serve, we should assume the leadership in reaffirming the role of the schools in character education.
- Boards should conduct a needs assessment in the community. We recognize that each community is unique. Therefore, each district should involve its community in determining the need for character education and the direction the program should take.
- Boards should be willing to set acceptable standards for behavior in the schools. We affirm the following statement made in the Violence and Vandalism Report published by CSBA in 1982 regarding lack of discipline:

  > If we have learned anything over the years, it is that it is almost impossible to impose standards. All groups that are going to be affected by the standards must "buy into them." Discipline and control policies should be developed and implemented by school personnel, parents, and students working together. Communications should not be left to chance. Discipline policy must give firm and positive direction. Local school rules and regulations must identify standards of behavior that are clear, concise, and easily understood by parents, teachers, and students. The ultimate goal should be to train students to have self-direction and self-control.[2]

- Boards of education should develop policies and guidelines to enable students to achieve the goals of character education.[3]

Herbert C. Mayer, when president of American Viewpoint, said that the starting point was to recognize that values were not caught and therefore must be taught. His organization developed and tested a successful character education course in Ossining, New York. One conclusion was that its approach should not be dogmatic or punitive. Although even this, Dr. Mayer said,

> *might be preferable to the moral vacuum which frequently exists.... Whatever the disadvantages of child training of past generations with regimentation and harsh discipline, those youngsters knew what was expected of them. They may not have understood why they were expected to do some things, but they knew that they had to do them or suffer the consequences. They had a code of behavior even though it may have been imposed on them. Today few of our youngsters have anything faintly resembling a code of morals. Literally, they do not know what is right or wrong.[4]*

Dr. Mayer went on to say that the actual teaching of values is not difficult. He listed four essential steps: "Identification of a value, examination of it, choice or rejection of it as related to one's point of view, and actual practice of it in everyday life."[5]

His American Viewpoint staff, working in cooperation with classroom teachers in the Ossining school system, developed a set of basic character education guidelines:

- That there was evident and imperative need for teaching moral and ethical values to growing children.
- That the classroom is one of the best situations in which such teaching can be done.
- That the teaching should be in the context of the Social Studies, not as an additional subject.
- That suitable materials must be found to supplement the regular curriculum.
- That the traditional method of "moralizing" is to be avoided.
- That specific values should be taught at the appropriate time in the development of children.
- That the program should combine real experience, vicarious experience, reading, studying, discussion, and practice.

97

- That teachers be encouraged to experiment and be alert to desirable teaching situations.
- That there must be direct teaching of values in order to have them take root and change behavior.[6]

Virginia Trevitt, whose high school ethics course is described in Chapter 4, captured her students' attention by appealing to the idealism that seems to characterize many young people. Her aim was to "create a new type of student who saw education as relevant to the needs of the world"—hence her theme, As I Am, So Is My Nation. She stressed the need for open discussion, for studying the lives of great men and women, and for encouraging students to test ethical concepts in their daily lives. Her methods are described in her book, *The American Heritage: Design for National Character*.[7]

SHOULD ETHICS BE A SEPARATE SUBJECT?

Many educators believe that ethical instruction should be woven into the overall curriculum rather than be treated as a separate subject. This may be a worthy ideal, and it certainly was the case many years ago in the days of the McGuffey Reader. "As recently as twenty-five years ago," stated Dr. John Silber in 1980, "citizenship education, that is, education of the child in morals and civic duty, was the central core and focus of all primary and secondary education.* It was what education was about."[8]

The problem with the idea that ethics should be woven into the curriculum is that this would entail a huge and expensive revision of most present school textbooks. If character education is as important as reading, writing, and arithmetic, as the authors insist, then why shouldn't it be taught specifically, systematically, and separately? Does our society really want citizens who have learned to read and write but have never learned to be honest and considerate?

---

* Dr. Silber is referring to citizenship education. The decline in emphasis on ethical instruction started before 1900.

The Character Education Curriculum, which has been described in previous pages, enables teachers to treat character as part of social studies and/or language arts. This does not, however, preclude references to behavior throughout the school day. The American Institute for Character Education recommends that this program be used for five or ten minutes each day in kindergarten; fifteen or twenty minutes each day, four days a week, for first through third grades; and twenty to thirty minutes a day, three times a week, for fourth through sixth grades. Teaching techniques include stories, Socratic questions, open discussion, role playing, art projects, case studies, posters, songs, and poems. The program stresses student participation, and students are encouraged to test the ethical concepts in their daily lives.

Professors Joseph Forcinelli and Thomas Engeman made a comparative study of several approaches to value education in public schools. Their conclusion was that "the Character Education Curriculum presents the most attractive choice for the value educator.... The instructional sophistication of the Character Education Curriculum is second to none in this area."[9]

Opponents of systematic instruction in character education often make the point that teachers teach character through their example and by inclusion of citizenship values in discussions of other topics. They maintain that this indirect form of teaching is sufficient. The authors of this book emphatically disagree. Seeing a person being honest or hearing a person telling the truth is not enough. Children must be exposed to the underlying concepts upon which the need for honesty and truth is based. Exposure to the reasons for these values cannot be left to chance; it must be systematic.

USING HISTORY TO TEACH CHARACTER

Examples from history and the study of the lives of great men and women is a method of teaching ethics that was once widely used in American schools and is still used in other countries. One reason that American schools no longer use history, according to

Benson and Engeman, is that "John Dewey expressly opposed it in *Democracy in Education.*"[10]

Plutarch's Lives, according to Benson,

> *includes comments on the virtues and vices of the subject of the biography;* The Lives of the Saints *has long been used in religious education. Military school curricula described the courageous exploits of their alumni, and the British public schools in England's nineteenth-century revival of morality brought back "old boys" (alumni) to the campus to encourage students to higher and more courageous ideals of public service. Religious orders commemorate their more pious deceased members; the stories of Lincoln's moral deeds can inspire young people who are interested in politics; and Parson Weems' biography of George Washington was historically inaccurate, but the stories it told may have helped many Americans to live better lives.* McGuffey's Readers, *widely employed in American public schools in the last century, include a number of historical examples of courage, honesty, gentleness, and other moral qualities."*

Before World War II, every Japanese schoolchild memorized a code of ethics, and this was reinforced with formal daily ethical instruction in the classroom. Instruction consisted chiefly of stories and biographical sketches.

Reed Irvine describes a typical text printed in Japan for use in Japanese schools in Hawaii:

> *The text began with a story that emphasized respect for parents and the importance of children avoiding actions which might bring disgrace to their families. This was followed by a chapter on Abraham Lincoln which emphasized his honesty, kindness, and sense of justice. Next came a biography of James A. Garfield, an inspiring story of his struggle to rise from the depths of poverty, a story that has probably not been read by any American school child (outside of Hawaii's Japanese schools) for several generations. This account*

of Garfield's life stressed the sacrifice made by his older brother to permit James to attend school, and it showed how James repaid his debt by his great diligence in both study and work. Other exemplary men of character portrayed in this text include Herbert Hoover, Admiral Togo, who won fame in the Russo-Japanese War, and the conqueror of yellow fever, Dr. Noguchi... [12]

One outstanding series of biographies parents and teachers can use as a tool for helping children understand basic personal values is called ValueTales. This program consists of twenty attractively illustrated books. Each book is about a historical figure and is written to emphasize one particular value or character trait: the life of Louis Pasteur teaches the value of believing in yourself; the life of Helen Keller illustrates determination; the story of the Wright brothers describes patience; and so forth.

WHAT LAYMEN CAN DO TO HELP YOUNG PEOPLE

Frequently, people who are not in education would like to encourage schools to do more in this regard but are not sure how to proceed.

The American system of public education is unique. In other countries, education is governed by professional educators or federal officials. The Tenth Amendment to the United States Constitution reserves the responsibility for public education to the states or to "the people." This democratic approach to education has produced a system which is usually responsive "to the people" at the local level.

Because of the democratic nature of our public schools, changes may be initiated from a variety of sources, including boards of education; superintendents; assistant superintendents; school principals; school advisory groups and parent-teacher associations; community groups such as business-education councils, chambers of commerce, service clubs, and crime task forces; parents; and teachers and other members of the staff.

Since there are many forces that mold the local schools, no single approach is best for all districts. In some districts, school boards have provided the leadership for starting character education. In other districts, it has been initiated by the superintendent or an assistant superintendent for instruction; elsewhere principals and teachers have provided the impetus. Board members or school administrators can usually recommend the best way to present and start the program successfully.

Community organizations with a personal relationship to educational leaders (perhaps the superintendent or school board member belongs to the Kiwanis or Rotary or Junior League Club) are usually an excellent starting point. Prominent business or community leaders may help to gain school interest.

It is highly desirable to involve school board and parent-teacher organizations since the entire community benefits from systematic character education in its schools. School superintendents, if they do not receive strong community support, have a tendency to refer community suggestions to their curriculum people. Curriculum specialists may reject such suggested programs because "they were not invented here."

VALUES CLARIFICATION

An approach to ethical instruction that has gained much attention and academic support is called Values Clarification or Moral Values Education. This approach was initiated in England and the United States in the early sixties and later became influential in Canada.

This approach to ethical instruction is significantly different from those mentioned in the first part of this chapter. Its advocates want to teach young people how to choose values but not which values to choose.

One of the most influential leaders in this movement is Sidney Simon, School of Education at the University of Massachusetts. Dr. Simon rejects what he regards as a fundamental error in traditional approaches to moral education—indoctrination. He sees this as an attempt by adults to impose values upon the young. Indoctrination, he believes, is not only ineffective but highly objectionable because it is based on the traditional principle that there are right and wrong ways of thinking and acting.

Professor Simon states, "None of us has the 'right' set of values to pass on to other people's children."[13]

Dr. Simon's approach, which he calls Values Clarification, is the most widely used moral values education program in American elementary and secondary schools. He starts with the conviction that traditional moral education is irrelevant in today's complex modern world. Dr. Simon writes:

> *The children of today are confronted by many more choices than in previous generations.*
>
> *Areas of confusion and conflict abound: politics, religion, love and sex, family, friends, drugs, materialism, race, work, aging and death, leisure time, school, and health. Each area demands decisions that yesterday's children were rarely called upon to make.[14]*

Values Clarification is concerned not with which values people develop but how they develop their values. The approach seeks to promote growth, freedom, and ethical maturity. The program asks parents, teachers, and other adults to start with the recognition that "there's no right or wrong answer to any question of value."[15]

Teachers are provided with classroom problems or dilemmas that are designed to help students discover their own values. In a typical exercise, the student is asked to answer questions such as:

1. *Which do you think is the most religious thing to do on a Sunday morning?*

    (a) Go to church and hear a very good preacher.
    (b) Listen to some classical music on the radio.
    (c) Have a big breakfast with the family.

2. *Which do you like the least?*

    (a) An uptight indoctrinator.
    (b) A cynical debunker.
    (c) A dull, boring fact giver.[16]

In another exercise, Simon requests parents and teachers to pose the following problem:

Your husband or wife is a very attractive person. Your best friend is very attracted to him or her. How would you want them to behave?

(a) Maintain a clandestine relationship so you wouldn't know about it.
(b) Be honest and accept the reality of the relationship.
(c) Proceed with a divorce.[17]

Critics of Values Clarification point out that the traditional response, "behave themselves," isn't even offered as an option.

"Values-clarification 'strategies,'" write Professors Bennett and Delattre,

are supposed to give students the greatest possible freedom of choice and knowledge of themselves and the world. By accepting the idea that there are no right or wrong answers to questions of morality and conduct, students learn that being clear about what one wants is all that is required to live well. But do such "strategies" really provide knowledge about the world and freedom of choice? Do they actually make for self-knowledge and ethical maturity and autonomy?... The first exercise, about the most religious thing to do on a Sunday morning, asks the student to think about what he wants and likes to do on Sunday mornings. Yet it introduces no other considerations, and implies that whatever the student thinks is religious thereby is religious.[18]

COGNITIVE MORAL DEVELOPMENT

Lawrence Kohlberg founded the Center for Moral Development at Harvard University. He, like Simon, is highly critical of traditional moral education, viewing it as useless and totalitarian. He too has "objected to the deliberate effort to

104

inculcate majority values... as a violation of the child's moral freedom."[19]

Dr. Kohlberg, however, believes that Simon's approach is too relativistic and leads students to the conclusion that ethical relativity is true. Kohlberg believes that relativism is scientifically incorrect.

Kohlberg calls his method Cognitive Moral Development and emphasizes the need for a sound theory on the development of moral reasoning. He traces his ideas to John Dewey and Jean Piaget and says that people's thinking about moral problems develops through specific stages. These stages of moral development are invariable and occur regardless of race or culture.

Kohlberg's six stages, briefly outlined, are:

Stage 1. Action is motivated by avoidance of punishment, and "conscience" is a non-rational fear of punishment.

Stage 2. Action is motivated by desire for reward or benefit. Possible guilt reactions are ignored and punishment viewed in a pragmatic manner.

Stage 3. Action is motivated by anticipation of disapproval of others, actual or imagined hypothetical.

Stage 4. Action is motivated by anticipation of dishonor, that is, institutionalized blame for failure of duty, and by guilt over concrete harm done to others.

Stage 5. Action is motivated by concern about maintaining respect of equals and of the community (assuming their respect is based on reason rather than emotions). Concern about own self-respect, that is, to avoid judging self as irrational, inconsistent, nonpurposeful.

Stage 6. Action is motivated by concern about self-condemnation for violating one's own principles. (Differentiates between community respect and self-respect.) Differentiates between self-respect for generally achieving rationality and self-respect for maintaining moral principles.[20]

Dr. Kohlberg emphasizes the child's right to freedom of choice. He believes that there is one universal, all-inclusive ethical principle—justice. People can be helped to move to higher stages of moral development but less than twenty percent of all adults ever develop beyond Stage 4.

Professor Kohlberg's typical classroom exercise is the moral dilemma. Dilemmas are intended to stimulate student discussion and enable students to move to higher stages of moral development.

A book listing some dilemmas, hypothetical dilemmas for use in moral discussions, has been prepared and is distributed by the Center for Moral Development. Here is a typical dilemma from this book:

"SWAPPING"

A number of married couples who knew each other were thinking of "swapping" (changing partners for sexual intercourse). The couples lived in the same neighborhood and knew each other quite well. They were people in their late thirties or early forties. They felt that they would like to have new sexual experiences. They felt that after being married for so long and having sex with the same person, sex had become quite dull.

1. *If all the couples agreed to it, would it be alright for them to change partners? Why or why not?*
2. *Recently there have been a number of "swapping" cases reported in the newspapers. The public's general reaction is very negative. Why do you think people react this way? Do you agree or disagree with them? Give your reasons.*
3. *If the couples had children, would this make any difference? What effect do you think "swapping" would have on the children?*
4. *What could some of the possible positive effects be?*
5. *What could some of the possible negative effects be?*[21]

Of the fifty dilemmas listed in the book, twenty-one are related to sexual conflicts—homosexuality, swapping, extramarital sex, etc. Other dilemmas mention My Lai, Daniel Barrigan, Daniel Ellsberg, women's liberation, kidney transplants, draft evasion, and abortion.

Professor Kohlberg makes the following comments about the use of dilemmas:

> *It is not always necessary that the matters discussed be ones of the immediate and real-life issues of the classroom. I have found that my hypothetical and remote but obviously morally real and challenging conflict situations are of intense interest to almost all adolescents and lead to lengthy debate among them. They are involving, because the adult right answer is not obviously at hand to discourage the child's own moral thought, as so often is the case.*[22]

DO THE VALUES CLARIFICATION APPROACHES WORK?

Professors Simon and Kohlberg and their colleagues have had great impact on professional educators but their methods have also aroused a great deal of controversy.

Are young people capable of developing a sound code of ethics without exposure to the ideas of the great philosophers and the accumulated wisdom of the ages? Some observers are convinced that what young people gain from these programs is contempt for authority and tradition.

Parent groups in several communities have been highly critical of Values Clarification and opposed its use in public schools. Richard A. Baer, Jr., Cornell University professor, provides the following information about opposition to Values Clarification:

> *Back in the mid-1960s, social scientists Louis E. Raths, Merrill Harmin, and Sidney B. Simon developed the teaching method known as Values Clarification, advertising it as an ideal way to deal with values*

without taking sides or indoctrinating students in one particular value position....

Parents did not react immediately. But when children began to report over dinner that class discussion had been about whether lying was sometimes permissible and whether they should always obey their parents, it wasn't long before groups of parents began to mobilize against Values Clarification.

Many of these parents were Christian fundamentalists. Their arguments were not couched in the sophisticated jargon of philosophy or social science, and sometimes emotions outstripped logic. But they left little doubt that they thought Values Clarification was teaching their children a kind of ethical relativism.

Instead of meeting such objections with solid arguments of their own, many educators attacked the objectors, dismissing their criticism as little more than a reactionary fundamentalist response to education innovation.... Over the past seven years, nonfundamentalist scholars from major universities—including Professors Kenneth A. Strike of Cornell, Alan L. Lockwood of the University of Wisconsin, and John S. Stewart, formerly of Michigan State University—have faulted Values Clarification on at least a dozen counts. The list of critics also includes William J. Bennett, recently appointed by President Reagan as chairman of the National Endowment for the Humanities, and Edwin J. Delattre, president of St. John's College in Annapolis. The major objections of these writers are virtually identical with those initially raised by religious fundamentalists and other parents' groups.

First, contrary to what its proponents claim, Values Clarification is not values-neutral. Even on the level of particular ethical decisions, where the authors try hard to be neutral, they succeed only partially. As Messrs. Bennett and Delattre point out, the approach used in

108

such Values Clarification strategies as Sidney Simon's "Priorities" "emphatically indoctrinates—by encouraging and even exhorting the student to narcissistic self-gratification."

And on the deeper level of what philosophers call "metaethics"—that is, critical analysis and theory about the nature of values as such—the claim to neutrality is entirely misleading. At this more basic level, the originators of Values Clarification simply assume that their own subjectivist theory of values is correct. By affirming the complete relativity of all values, they in effect equate values with personal tastes and preferences. If parents object to their children using pot or engaging in premarital sex, the theory behind Values Clarification makes it appropriate for the child to respond, "But that's just your value judgment. Don't force it on me."

Furthermore, Values Clarification indoctrinates students in ethical relativism, for its proponents push their own position on their captive student audiences and never suggest that thoughtful people may choose alternatives. Sidney Simon, Howard Kirschenbaum, and other Values Clarification authors repeatedly belittle teachers of traditional values. Such teachers, they claim, "moralize," "preach," "manipulate," and "whip the child into line." Their positions are "rigid" and they rely on "religion and other cultural truisms."

The second major fault, according to the University of Wisconsin's Alan Lockwood, is that "a substantial proportion of the content and methods of Values Clarification constitutes a threat to the privacy rights of students and their families." To be sure, the method permits students to say "I pass" when the teacher asks them to complete such open-ended sentences as "If I had 24 hours to live....," ""Secretly I wish...," or "My parents are usually...," but many of these "projective techniques" are designed in such a fashion, Mr.

Lockwood claims, that students often will realize too late that they have divulged more about themselves and their families than they wish or feel is appropriate in a public setting. Moreover, the method itself incorporates pressure toward self-disclosure.

A third criticism of Values Clarification is that by presupposing very specific views about human nature and society, it becomes a kind of "religious" position in its own right which competes directly with other religious views.[23]

Reo M. Christenson, professor of political science at Miami University in Oxford, Ohio, is another outspoken critic of Values Clarification. He writes:

Let me be blunt: Given their meager life experience, their myopic vision and necessarily immature judgment, teenagers lack the ability to formulate independently a sound value system. It is foolish and naive to expect them to. Too many students during these sessions will try to rationalize values that promote their freedom to do as they please.

Students need to know and have a right to know what thoughtful and responsible people over the centuries have learned about living. If we fail to tell them, we do them a profound disservice.[24]

The Values Clarification approaches are controversial. Some educators believe that they are the *best* way to help young people, whereas others believe these approaches are unproductive or actually counterproductive. The authors of this book tend to agree with the latter viewpoint.

Needed to resolve this dispute are careful research studies that concentrate on results obtained by the various approaches to ethical instruction. These studies should concentrate on desirable outcomes such as reduced vandalism and improved attendance, scholarship, and student behavior.

Chapter 9

BENEFITS FROM CHARACTER EDUCATION

If you can be well without health, you may be happy without virtue.

Edmund Burke

Systematic character education in primary and secondary schools is a remarkable bargain for the entire community. Students benefit by acquiring positive attitudes and habits that enhance their self-esteem and make their lives happier and more productive. Teachers' work becomes easier and more satisfying when they achieve greater classroom discipline. Parents are pleased when their children learn to be more courteous, considerate, and productive. School administrators welcome the improvements in discipline, attendance, scholarship, and student and teacher morale, as well as sometimes significant reductions in school vandalism.

Business people, increasingly concerned with the costs and problems they are experiencing in hiring young people who are poorly trained and disciplined, welcome programs that improve youthful attitudes and behavior.

The Character Education Curriculum, created by the American Institute for Character Education in San Antonio and distributed by the American Institute and the Thomas Jefferson Research Center, seems to be one of the best programs available at the elementary school level. Some of the positive results obtained by this program are described in Chapter 4. Although the authors are not aware of any longitudinal research to determine the long-term influence of such programs on young people, there is good reason to believe that early ethical instruction does have a lifetime influence on many, if not most, of those who receive it. The fact that crime and delinquency were much, much lower in the days when schools did place greater emphasis on ethical instruction is most encouraging.

EVALUATION OF THE CHARACTER EDUCATION CURRICULUM

Several organizations have conducted formal evaluations of the Character Education Curriculum in an effort to determine objectively the program's benefits. One such study was conducted by the American Institute for Research. This study compared a group of children who had been exposed to the program for two years with a comparable control group. Data were gathered at kindergarten, third-grade, and sixth-grade levels. The report states:

> *Students in the treatment group at the kindergarten and third grade levels showed a clear advantage in the performance of character-related behaviors over students who were not exposed to the program. The beneficial effects appeared across the entire range of objectives of the curriculum, but were most clearly and convincingly evident in the areas of honesty and truthfulness, kindness, generosity, and helpfulness....*
> *Results of the sixth grade level were dramatically different from those for the lower grades. There is no support for a favorable judgment on the impact of the AICE curriculum at this level.... Examination of the sixth grade results leads to many explanations which at this time are purely speculative. Some of these include: (1) the AICE curriculum may not have been appropriate for the sixth grade; (2) the research design of the study may have been inappropriate for the*

curriculum; and (3) the instruments used in the study may not have been suitable for the sixth grade group.[1]

The above evaluation was on the first-generation character education materials. The entire program has since been revised and improved, and the sixth-grade level received major revisions.

THE DADE COUNTY EVALUATION

Several school districts have conducted formal evaluations of the Character Education Curriculum. One such study was conducted by Dade County schools in Florida. Two professors from Trinity University in San Antonio were employed to provide an independent, in-depth study of the program's success in ten Dade County schools.

The evaluation was accomplished by sampling the reactions of teachers, students, and parents. To secure information as free from bias as possible, respondents were told, "We did not write the Character Education program. We are not selling it. We are here to find out what you really think about the program."[2] Respondents were also assured their answers would be confidential.

The final conclusion from this evaluation was:

The findings from the Character Education evaluation were indeed very impressive. The attitudes of the administrators, teachers, parents, and students were very positive.... Many merits were enumerated.... All persons involved in the program thought it beneficial and strongly believed the program should be continued and expanded.[3]

Teachers interviewed generally said they liked the program and felt that it had been responsible for changes in both themselves and their students. Following are some of the remarks of teachers using Character Education Curriculum:

"My first graders have increased their vocabulary so much, it has really helped."

"It gives you a social studies program with everything right before you. It saves much time."

"Character Education has taught my students to be more responsible toward themselves and others."

"... of all my years of teaching, I feel this has been my most profitable year, because of Character Education."

"Stealing has virtually stopped in my classroom. Believe me, it really was a problem before."[4]

Tables 3–5 summarize the responses of selected samples of students, teachers, and parents to the questionnaire:

Table 3
RESPONSES TO PARENT QUESTIONNAIRE
(N-31)

	None	Little	Some	Much	Very Much	Total % of 3,4,&5
Do you approve of your child learning Character Education in school?	0	0	0	5	95	100%
Has your child ever talked about the Character Education Program or something he has learned from it?	29	10	14	33	14	61%
Do you think the program has been responsible for any changes you have noticed in your child's behavior?	10	14	33	19	24	76%
Do you think the Character Education Program should be continued?	0	0	0	5	95	100%

Table 4
RESPONSES TO TEACHER QUESTIONNAIRE
Grades K–5 (N-31)

	None	Little	Some	Much	Very Much	Total % of 3,4,&5
Do you think the Character Education materials have been responsible for changes in the behavior of your students?	0	10	45	29	16	90%
Do you enjoy teaching Character Education?	0	6	6	29	58	94%
Does Character Education improve student responsibility?	0	6	32	29	32	94%
Do you feel the Character Education program is worthwhile?	0	0	3	26	71	100%

Table 5
RESPONSES TO STUDENT QUESTIONNAIRE
Grades 3–5(N-362)

	None	Little	Some	Much	Very Much	Total % of 3,4,&5
Do you enjoy learning about Character Education?	1	3	9	22	65	96%
Do you think it is wise to be honest?	3	3	5	10	79	94%
Do you believe that laws and rules are necessary?	1	1	4	10	83	97%
Do you think Character Education is worthwhile?	1	2	12	34	51	97%

SAN ANTONIO INDEPENDENT SCHOOL DISTRICT EVALUATION

In January 1982 the San Antonio Independent School District made a study of the effect of the Character Education Curriculum on students' self-concept. District personnel administered pretests of the Piers-Harris Children's Self-

Concept Scale to three experimental schools and compared results with those obtained from three control schools. The schools were selected on the basis of socioeconomic status and ethnicity. A total of 507 students participated in the study.

Four months later, in May 1982, posttests were administered in the same schools. In those schools that used the character education program, the gains are recorded in Table 6.

Table 6
STUDENT IMPROVEMENT

Elementary Schools	Percentage of Students Who Improved
Knox	
Grade 3	50%
Grade 4	57%
Grade 5	60%
Stewart	
Grade 3	72%
Grade 4	71%
Woodlaw	
Grade 3	55%
Grade 4	45%
Grade 5	52%

From pre- to posttest intervention, the experimental school scores ranged from 26 percent to 65 percent improvement, whereas the scores of those schools that did not use the program, the control schools, ranged from 9 percent to 29 percent.

Further research is currently under way to show the correlation between improved self-concept (via Character Education) and improved academic achievement, attendance (ADA), and student behavior.

According to Amy Jo Baker, social studies curriculum specialist in the San Antonio Independent School District and coordinator of this evaluation, "Since significant gains were made after a semester of using the Character Education Curriculum, it can be expected that even greater improvement can take place using the program for an entire school year."[5]

The San Antonio Independent School District also distributed questionnaires to parents, teachers, and students in ten

116

elementary schools using the Character Education Curriculum. The key results are logged in Tables 7–9.

Table 7
PARENT QUESTIONNAIRE

	Yes	No	No Opinion
Do you approve of your child learning Character Education in school?	93%	0	7%
Do you think Character Education is worthwhile?	85%	0	15%
Do you think the Character Education program should be continued?	85%	0	15%

Table 8
TEACHER QUESTIONNAIRE

	Yes	No	No Opinion
Does the Character Education program help you in teaching responsibility to your students	92%	2%	6%
Are students interested in the Character Education instruction?	94%	1%	5%
Has there been any change in classroom behavior such as class disruption, cursing, etc.?	66%	19%	15%
Would you like to have the Character Education program continued?	81%	3%	16%

Table 9
STUDENT QUESTIONNAIRE

Do you like the Character Education program?	93%	2%	5%
Do you use the Character Education ideas away from school, such as at home and on the playground?	73%	17%	10%
Do you think that Character Education is worthwhile?	8%	7%	6%

SPECIFIC BENEFITS

Educators using the Character Education Curriculum report the following specific benefits:

IMPROVED CLASSROOM DISCIPLINE

Improving classroom discipline is one of teachers' most elusive problems, and evaluating success in this area is one of the toughest challenges an evaluator can face. Nevertheless, evidence from many classrooms shows that the Character Education Curriculum can make a significant difference. Crockett Elementary School in Harlingen, Texas, for example, found that during the first six-week period it used the program, "The number of students referred to the office for discipline dropped from forty to fifty each week to an average of one each day."[6]

Michael Martin, one of the teachers at Valley Vista Elementary School in Chula Vista, California, told a group of school administrators that "Disciplinary problems almost disappeared in the classroom, in the cafeteria, and on the playground soon after the program was introduced."[7]

REDUCED THEFT, VANDALISM, AND VIOLENCE

Beatrice Bowles, principal of Public School 63 in Indianapolis, gave the following report:

> *The building resembled a school in a riot area; $3,500 worth of glass had been broken between September and June; the pupils were rude, discourteous, and insolent. They had no school pride, very poor self-image, and were disgruntled to attend school. Since we started Character Education, there has been less than $100 worth of glass breakage and school attitudes have greatly improved. Students are now respectful and cooperative and there is a feeling of one for all and all for one.*[8]

Meliton Lopez, assistant superintendent in Chula Vista, reported that schools there tested the Character Education program for three years. When the cost per month for vandalism for the test period was compared with vandalism for the thirty months before using the program, it was found that the monthly cost had been reduced to one-thirteenth of the previous figure.

IMPROVED STUDENT ATTENDANCE

Some schools using the Character Education program report sizable improvements in attendance. Administrators at John J. Pershing Elementary School in San Antonio reported that they "have the statistics which will show that the ADA (average daily attendance) has increased over the last year and a half from 85 percent to an average of 95 percent."[9]

Other schools using the program report attendance improvements ranging from zero to more than 10 percent.

IMPROVED SCHOLARSHIP

Scholarship, like discipline, is not easily measured, but many teachers are convinced that the Character Education Curriculum does improve scholarship as well as discipline. The dramatic scholarship improvements in Modesto, California, schools cannot be attributed solely to the Character Education Curriculum, but Assistant Superintendent James Enochs says that the character program was certainly a major factor.

Beatrice Bowles said that after six years of using the program in every classroom, "Our children are well behaved, courteous, and with few exceptions, achieving at maximum potential.... There is a noticeable improvement in the attitudes, behavior, and achievement of our children, now sixth graders, who have been in the program the entire six school years."[10]

IMPROVED STUDENT ATTITUDES

Almost all teachers using the Character Education Curriculum report improvements in student attitudes. "We're spending less time counseling individual students," writes Jim Casey, principal of Benjamin Franklin School in Champaign, Illinois; "discipline referrals have drastically decreased; attendance has vastly improved; vandalism is virtually nonexistent; and students demonstrate real school spirit."[11]

IMPROVED VERBAL SKILLS

Open uncritical discussion on a subject that all children are familiar with—their own behavior—can be very helpful for students who, in other subjects, have little to say. The result in some instances is greatly improved verbal skills.

Lawrence James, principal of 59th Street Elementary School in Los Angeles, an inner-city school, says that many of his teachers like the program because it encourages students to talk openly.

Scott Love, one of his sixth-grade teachers, said, "A lot of our kids tend to be real physical because their verbal experience has been below par. If they can't express themselves verbally, they will very often do it physically."[12]

IMPROVED TEACHER MORALE

Beatrice Bowles' school in Indianapolis had mostly black students from very low-income families. More than half of her teachers were white. After six years' experience with the Character Education Curriculum, she discovered that she had very little teacher turnover. One substitute white teacher said that she would rather teach at Public School 63 than at any other school in Indianapolis.

The following comment comes from David Fairchild Elementary School in Dade County, Florida: "Perhaps the most important difference has been in the attitudes of teachers: at last we can do something about children's attitudes and values; we can do positive things instead of just lamenting the fact that many children have socially unacceptable values. Teachers feel good about taking positive steps to improve children's values, and the Character Education materials help them do this."[13]

INCREASED COMMUNITY SUPPORT

Americans perceive the problem of discipline as one of the most important problems facing public schools. The thirteenth Gallup poll of the public attitude toward public schools included the following question: "Would you favor or oppose instruction in the schools that would deal with values and ethical behavior?" For parents with children in public schools, 73 percent were in

120

favor of ethical instruction. Studies of parent attitudes toward character education in Modesto, Dade County, Allegheny County, San Antonio, and elsewhere have consistently found a very high level of parent support for character education.[14]

DISCIPLINE AIDS SCHOLARSHIP

Several educational studies have identified a positive correlation between discipline and academic performance. Given recent negative trends in scholarship, this relationship between discipline and performance has great significance.

Numerous studies show that academic achievement in American schools has been going downhill since the early 1960s. Solveig Eggerz, in her excellent essay "Why Our Public Schools Are Failing," provides the following information:

The decline in Scholastic Aptitude Test scores, which began in 1963, took its most dramatic dip in three years in 1980 when the average verbal test score was 424 compared to 427 in 1979 and 478 in 1963.

The 1963 overall test score of 502 in math sank to 466 in 1980, down from 467 in 1979.

Even more shocking than the general decline is the drop in achievement among highest scoring students. From 1979 to 1980 the number of students getting the highest SAT scores—over 750—fell from 2,650 to 1,892 in verbal areas and from 9,059 to 7,675 in math.

In fact, the number of students scoring better than 650 on college entrance exams has dropped dramatically since the early 1970s, by 46 percent. From 1972 to 1980 those scoring better than 650 on the verbal part of the SAT dropped from 53,794 to 29,019....

A Ford Foundation study concludes that as many as 64 million Americans lack the reading and writing abilities needed for today's technologies....

121

A National Science Foundation study from 1980 warns that most Americans are headed "toward virtual scientific and technological illiteracy." The report says, "More students than ever are dropping out of science and mathematics courses after the 10th grade, and this trend shows no signs of abating."[15]

Lack of discipline in American schools leads to violence, vandalism, theft, drugs, alcohol, and reduced academic achievement, and also deprives those students who want to study of a peaceful environment in which to do so.

According to a recent study by James S. Coleman, schools with more homework, less absenteeism, and an *orderly environment* have higher achievement regardless of the family background of the students.[16]

A study by Professor Ronald Edmonds of the Harvard Graduate School of Education concluded that effective schools had principals who were active leaders, an *orderly climate,* an emphasis on basic skills, standardized tests to measure skills, and teachers who have high expectations for all students.[17]

In a book entitled *15,000 Hours: Secondary Schools and Their Effects on Children,* English researchers report on a thorough examination of the British secondary school system. This study concluded, "Schools do indeed have an important impact on children's development and it does matter which school a child attends."[18]

When schools in poor neighborhoods in London were compared for performance, the study showed that some schools were much better than others. Which schools were better? Those schools that maintained an *orderly environment.* Teachers in those schools expected results, and assigned and checked homework regularly.[19]

A somewhat similar study in Dallas by the *Dallas Times Herald* found that additional money, class size, or teacher experience appeared not to affect student achievement.

During the past five years, according to the *Times Herald* report, the school district has spent more than $47 million to try to improve reading and math scores of poor, low-achieving students. Yet Superintendent Linus Wright admits that this costly effort has had little or no impact on student achievement.

The study concentrated on performance in eight of the Dallas district's poorest, mostly black elementary schools. Academic achievement in these eight schools ranged from very good at Wheatley, where most students were reading better than the average pupil nationwide, to poor at Colonial Elementary School, where test scores were the lowest in the district.

The most significant factor explaining the different performances in these two otherwise similar schools was not dollar expenditures per pupil, teacher color or teacher experience, but the quality of leadership. Superintendent Wright said a good principal is "the single, most important factor" in improving pupil achievement in the schools.

Principals who were able to establish discipline and high expectations were the ones whose students rated high in achievement in the schools.

Wheatley had established a tradition of high standards of behavior and had few disciplinary problems. Colonial, on the other hand, had students who fought on their way to school, all day at school, and on their way home. Their principal said that she had to devote virtually all of her time at Colonial trying to establish discipline.[20]

RESPONSIBLE BEHAVIOR DOES PAY

Students who develop a positive code of conduct and a healthy self-image not only will behave better in school, but in most cases will also become healthier, happier, more productive adults.

Many distinguished philosophers have pointed out the connection between virtuous behavior and true success—true happiness. Edmund Burke, whose quotation appears at the beginning of this chapter, is one example of this viewpoint.

Here are some similar statements by other great minds:

Were I not to follow the straight road for its straightness, I should follow it for having found by experience that in the end it is commonly the happiest and most useful track.

Michel Montaigne

If rascals knew the advantages of virtue, they would become honest men.

Benjamin Franklin

It is not the brains that matter most, but that which guides them—the character, the heart, generous qualities, progressive ideas.

Fedor Mikhailovich Dostoevski

No man is free who is not master of himself.

Epictetus

There is no truth more thoroughly established than that there exists in the course of Nature, an indissoluble union between virtue and happiness.

George Washington

Chapter 10

THE EDUCATIONAL PENDULUM IS SWINGING

There is one thing stronger than all the armies in the world, and that is an idea whose time has come.

Victor Hugo

In 1975 Howard Flieger, editor of *U.S. News & World Report,* said on his editorial page, "Is instruction in morals and ethics becoming more popular in the schools? There are some faint signs of it.... History makes a truism of Mr. Goble's statement that a society cannot survive without a workable system of values."[1] Unfortunately, this editorial seemed to arouse little interest or attention.

Several years later, however, when Marvin Stone, the new editor of *U.S. News & World Report,* wrote an editorial titled "Are Ethics on the Way Back?" the response was very different. The Thomas Jefferson Research Center received more than five hundred letters of inquiry about ethical instruction. That response dramatically confirmed Mr. Stone's statement that "it has become permissible to speak, write, and think about 'ethics.' That represents a healthy advance over very recent times when anyone who talked in such terms was regarded as naive."[2]

This editorial point of view, however, seems not to have influenced news articles in the *U.S. News & World Report.* Every month or so the magazine has an article on crime or violence or delinquency. Usually the articles include interviews and quotations from prominent scholars, psychologists, sociologists, and so forth. Not once in these articles have we found any reference to the lack of ethical instruction as a possible reason for exploding crime and violence.

The December 15, 1981, issue, for example, carried the article "Troubled Teenagers," which cited shocking statistics on crime, suicide, illegitimacy, and alcoholism. Several "experts" were interviewed to find out what was wrong, but not one of them mentioned that our schools and colleges had virtually stopped teaching ethics.

Nevertheless, the idea that schools and colleges and other institutions must place greater emphasis on efforts to teach ethical values is gaining acceptance. The many statements from prominent Americans which appear throughout this book show that this is so. The growing list of advocates now includes people like Chief Justice Burger and his administrative assistant Mark Cannon; Steve Muller, president of Johns Hopkins; Terrel Bell, secretary of education; John Silber, president of Boston University; John Howard, president of Rockford Institute; Bill Honig, California state superintendent of public instruction; Derek Bok, president of Harvard; and many, many others.

In the summer of 1973, Benson and Engeman tried to test the reactions of their colleagues in the social science faculties of the six colleges that compose the Claremont Colleges. Of fifty-plus respondents, they found that a clear majority favored ethical instruction. "Although many thought that it would do little good because larger social and intellectual forces are at work, the majority said that if it could be done in a nondogmatic manner, they would favor it."[3]

Benson and Engeman make the following report regarding England and Europe:

In England there is much greater support for individual ethics among intellectuals than there is in America. The Journal of Moral Education, *established in 1971, serves as a focal point for intellectual effort in ethical education. In addition, research units located at both Oxford and Cambridge Universities have done basic and applied research in ethical education. On the Continent, several countries are developing moral*

126

education programs for their public schools. Therefore, it is obviously not impossible for contemporary intellectuals to support ethical reform.[4]

Magazine and newspaper articles and editorials on ethical instruction in the schools seem to be on the increase. The authors have a growing file of such articles. Somewhat typical is an article from the February 22, 1982, issue of the *Wall Street Journal*. The title of the article is "Teaching Morality in the Public Schools" and its author, Terry Eastland, is editor of the *Virginia-Pilot* newspaper in Norfolk. Here are typical comments from this article:

> *It has been 20 years since the Supreme Court declared in Engel vs. Vitale that state-sponsored public school prayer violates the Constitution.... Proponents of school prayer say that crime, racial conflict, drug abuse, and sexual promiscuity, among other social problems, have intensified since the Engel decision.... Opponents of social prayer typically deride the idea that prayer might be thus efficacious....*

> *Sociologists may speculate about the cause of these problems, but fundamentally they result from a widespread absence in young people of a basic morality. This morality consists of, among other things, honesty, fairness, respect for law, courage, diligence, and respect for others. These qualities are commonly regarded as part of the Judeo-Christian ethic, but not its exclusive property....*

> *For more than two thousand years, Western nations have transmitted this basic morality to each new generation. The means of propagation have typically been the family, the church, and the schools. In the U.S., the public schools have been assigned the major share of the responsibility. But in the past two decades, the schools increasingly have failed to do this job....*

Everyone interested in the public schools should begin reviewing what is taught or failing to be taught in their schools, with a view toward making sure that the basic morality is recovered and instilled in the latest generation of students.... [5]

In Chapter 2 the authors summarized two surveys that concluded that character education was badly neglected in American schools. One of these, the Pohorlak report, was made in 1967, and the report by Dr. Klotz in 1968. A third survey, published in 1977 by Research for Better Schools, headquartered in Philadelphia, provided encouraging evidence that schools were rediscovering the importance of ethical instruction. [6]

The third report was based on a survey of state educational agencies which sought to discover whether "educators are prepared to meet the challenge of guiding youth (and adults) toward civic ethics." Forty-six states responded to the survey questions, which were designed to discover what were the current ideas and practices, if any, in ethical-citizenship education. The report concluded:

Since 1970, educators have increasingly attended to what many describe as a crisis in American character: the absence of values as a guide for personal behavior in both public and private life....

The popular mandate for public education to intervene in this crisis of character in youth and adults is also growing. Public opinion polls indicate that 67 percent of Americans feel that schools should share responsibility for the ethical behavior of children (Gallup, 1976); two of the most influential educational associations of the country have asserted the need for Ethical-Citizenship Education (ECE) in the schools (Hill and Wallace, 1976); and a majority of states are now engaged in polling local school community sentiment regarding ECE in the schools. [7]

SCHOOL BOARD ASSOCIATION REPORT

More recent evidence that the pendulum is swinging back toward greater emphasis on character education is provided by two reports published by the California School Board Association. The first report is "Task Force Report on Student Violence and Vandalism," published in September 1980. The report says that violence and vandalism are epidemic in our society and mentions four changes in society that contributed to the increase in violence:

(1) The breakdown of the home and family unit.
(2) The lack of self-discipline in children as well as the absence of control over their behavior by responsible adults.
(3) The growing power of television to influence viewers toward imitating violent behavior.
(4) Disrespect for the law and lack of effective legal penalties and strict enforcement.[8]

Although this report mentions lack of discipline as an important reason for exploding violence and vandalism, there is no mention in the list of suggested solutions of systematic character education as one way to achieve discipline and reduce violence and vandalism.

Approximately two years later, in 1982, a second California School Board Association task force concluded that character education is essential if California schools are to expect their students to be well behaved. This report, prepared by the Character Education Task Force of the California School Board Association, is titled "A Reawakening: Character Education and the Role of the School Board Member." Two paragraphs summarize the report:

The task force urges California School Board Association to continue to study the role of public schools in the development of character education. We further urge every school board to address this challenge which has become a crucial concern in our society.

In answer to those who say we are doing a character education curriculum right along, we question whether this is indeed being done. Somehow, we need to make the distinction between what we hope *is happening in the classroom and what is indeed happening.*[9]

POLITICAL EFFORTS TO ENCOURAGE CHARACTER EDUCATION

There have been several political efforts to encourage schools to emphasize ethics. Charles E. Bennett, a Florida congressman, held several hearings on the subject and introduced a bill, HR12399, to provide federal grants to assist elementary and secondary schools to carry on programs to teach the principles of citizenship and ethics.

On April 24, 1979, Congressman Bennett, speaking to the United States Congressional Subcommittee on Elementary, Secondary, and Vocational Education, made the following statement:

In 1977, persons under 18 in our country accounted for 41 percent of the arrests for serious crimes, although that age group (minus those under 10) was but 15 percent of the population.... I believe that this deterioration is due in large part to the failure of our schools to provide an adequate education in the field of good citizenship and what it means to our society and to each of us individually. This failure by the schools— at a time when family life is becoming increasingly fragmented—is giving us a new generation of Americans no longer guided by the ethical principles that have made our nation great."[10]

In California, State Senator Albert Rodda held several hearings to encourage character instruction in schools. In 1980 he formed the "Senate Select Committee on School Finance and Character Education." That committee published a report summarizing its several hearings as well as "A Compendium of Character Education Programs in California Public Schools."[11]

The California State Assembly passed AB399 on June 25, 1981, by a 52 to 23 vote. The bill spelled out values that should be included in public school instructional materials. Among these values were:

> *Honesty, acceptance of responsibility, respect for the individuality of others, respect for the responsibility inherent in being a parent or in a position of authority, the role of the work ethic in achieving personal goals, universal values of right and wrong, respect for property, the importance of the family unit, the principles of the free market economy, the importance of respecting the law, etc.*[12]

AB399 was rejected by the California Senate. Opponents said that although the aim was laudable, it was bad practice to put into law some vaguely worded doctrinal concepts. They were afraid that the measure would open a Pandora's box of doctrines required to be taught.

When Assemblyman William R. Leonard was questioned about what existing shortcomings his bill sought to remedy, he responded: "A trend by textbook publishers to put out bland textbooks that don't say anything about anything."

MARYLAND STATE COMMISSION

Maryland is apparently the first state in recent times to appoint a state commission on values. On May 16, 1978, Governor Harry Hughes approved Senate Joint Resolution 64, which created the Values Education Commission "to identify and assess ongoing programs in morals and values education in the schools of Maryland. And to formulate recommendations that would reinforce 'our traditional adherence and devotion to high standards of moral and ethical conduct' in personal and public life."

In creating the commission, the general assembly noted the widespread recognition of the breakdown "in the normal standards of individual behavior and violations of public trust" and a sense of helplessness about how to improve the situation. It said, "The elementary school is the appropriate place," to encourage "ideals and desirable personal and public conduct." In these early days, students form their values, attitudes, and conduct that will be the basis for their personal character and behavior as citizens.

Values education, the Maryland General Assembly noted, "should be continued in junior and senior high school."

A preliminary report from the Maryland Values Education Commission, dated July 30, 1979, states, "The commission takes the view that public schools are appropriate, indeed necessary, institutions in a democratic society for defining and encouraging character and citizenship values. The schools cannot supplant the role played by the family and religion in values education, but they can reinforce positive attitudes and behavior and counteract negative influences on the students."[13]

One interesting facet of the Maryland commission's effort is the fact that although the twenty-two commission members represent a wide political spectrum, they all managed to agree on a list of eighteen character and citizenship values.

One member of the bipartisan commission is Ernest LeFevre, president of the nonprofit Ethics and Public Policy Center. He was the center of sharp controversy when named by President Reagan as assistant secretary of state for human rights. He withdrew after being rejected by the U.S. Senate, which claimed that he was too sympathetic to right-wing dictatorships. At the other end of the commission's ideological spectrum, Toni Parker, a specialist in remedial programs for Montgomery County Schools, calls herself "super-ultra-liberal."[14]

MICHIGAN

Activities of school officials in Michigan provide additional evidence that ethical instruction is on the way back. "Education in Moral Values in Michigan" is the title of a report on a survey taken in the fall of 1967 by the Michigan State Board of Education. The questionnaire, sent to all school superintendents in the state, asked four questions:

1. *What is being done presently in your school district in regard to the moral aspects of education, particularly in regard to developing self-respect, respect for others, and respect for citizenship and authority in general?*
2. *What do you feel are the needs of the schools in your district in regard to this aspect of education?*
3. *What are the plans being made in your district or the programs being instituted in regard to meeting these needs?*
4. *What are your recommendations for better meeting these needs in the future?*[15]

Of the 552 school districts in the state, 269 responded (48 percent). However, since 22 of the 30 school districts with over 10,000 responded, the survey covered the majority of Michigan youngsters. The most important conclusion, says the report, "is the expression of obvious concern. Nearly everyone who reacted to this survey said that we need to be more concerned with the problem of the moral aspects of education. In no case did anyone say that he felt that this was not an important area of education."

A number of the educators said the need was urgent, and nearly all of them said schools should be doing more than they are doing at present. Many superintendents asked that teachers be shown better ways to deal with moral values and suggested that teacher training institutes tend to neglect this important area of education. A number mentioned the need for better teaching materials. In-service training was suggested many times.

Several of the responses mentioned the connection between lack of self-respect and lack of respect for others. It was apparent from the questionnaires that the majority of those responding felt that students did not have enough respect for authority.

Although the survey responses showed general recognition of the need for teaching children responsibility, the survey also revealed that "educators are better prepared to describe needs in this area in general than they are to describe specifically what they plan to do. A large number of educators say that they have no specific plans."[16]

Shortly after the task force report, the Michigan State Board of Education adopted a resolution on moral values and value systems, which stated:

133

We, the members of the State Board of Education, believe strongly—

That to function as responsible citizens in our complex world, each individual should have available not only "the facts" but a sound set of values upon which to base his decisions; and that each youngster should be aided in making his choice of values not only by his parents and church, but by the schools... [17]

VIRGINIA

Virginia is another state that has recently expressed concern for ethical instruction. In February 1981 the Virginia legislature passed a resolution that started thus: "Virginians are in substantial agreement regarding a number of ethical qualities judged necessary to civilized society, to democratic self-government, and to the prospering of the body politic...." The full text of this resolution is found in Chapter 5.

ILLINOIS

In December 1982, Donald G. Gill, Illinois state superintendent of schools, submitted a report on values education to the Illinois State Board of Education. This was the result of Dr. Gill's earlier request to the Illinois Curriculum Council to work with him "in developing a program for identifying commonly held democratic values, as a step toward a major curriculum effort intended to revitalize the teaching of values in our schools."[18] The report said:

The values which undergird our society have stood the test of time and have been the basis for the formation of other governments throughout the world. Even our adversaries have publicly espoused them as their own, despite their poor performance in implementing them. It is apparent that understanding and acceptance are

134

necessary ingredients to appropriate behavior; ignorance and shallow commitment lead only to lip service. It is therefore understandable that a traditional responsibility of education has been to instruct children in their rights and responsibilities in our free society.[19]

The report goes on to quote an excellent statement by William J. Bennett from the January 7, 1980, issue of *Newsweek:*

Civilization's values are learned. Children are not born with an instinct for democracy or citizenship. Civility, probity, a disinterested concern for the well-being of others are not part of the natural order. Efforts must be made by each generation of adults, for each generation of children, to bring them to an understanding of a spiritual inheritance that is their birthright but that doesn't come with birth. Free, responsible, thoughtful people do not emerge naturally or by accident. Rather, such people are the result of the intentions and efforts of parents, teachers, communities, and society at large. This requires that at all times we consciously nurture and support those institutions, practices, and traditions that move civilization along and provide new participants in it.[20]

Dr. Gill's project has not gained universal acceptance. An editorial in the *Chicago Sun-Times,* December 11, 1981, said, "State Education Superintendent Donald Gill wants to set up a program to teach moral and democratic values in the schools. That may sound like apple pie, but we think it is a lemon.... Why can't the schools just impart knowledge and let it go at that?... They don't need indoctrination in values; they need to learn how to read, write, cipher, and reason."[21]

SALT LAKE CITY

Salt Lake Superintendent of Schools M. Donald Thomas is another action-oriented advocate for what he describes as "education focused on producing moral conduct." He says that the idea is certainly not new and that in the earlier days "moral education was a major part of the school experience."

Salt Lake City schools recently received a grant from the Danforth Foundation to develop a "moral education" program for South High School in Salt Lake City.[22]

PORTLAND, MAINE

During the summer of 1980 a team of twelve Portland, Maine, teachers and coordinators worked on the Portland Project on Character and Community. Their task was to develop a pilot project that could be used in the junior and senior high schools to help students develop some simple and basic traits that lead to good character.

John Johnson, social studies teacher at King Junior High School, says that "respect for other people, seeking fairness, being an honest person are the kinds of qualities that lead to a happy, well-adjusted life."[23] Peter R. Greer, Portland superintendent of schools, believes that students have a right to have all the help they can get in order to grow up to become responsible, happy people. He says, "It is increasingly clear that our nation's students will continue to suffer if educational leaders cannot find the courage and good sense to keep only the best and most qualified teachers in the nation's classrooms."[24]

SUPERINTENDENTS AND SCHOOL BOARD MEMBERS ENDORSE CHARACTER EDUCATION

During 1982 the Thomas Jefferson Research Center, in cooperation with the Center for Leadership Development, sponsored four leadership workshops for superintendents and board members in Northern and Southern California school districts. The workshops included a discussion of the advantages of systematic character education in the schools.

The response of the participants to the presentations on

character education was positive in every way. Before the sessions, during the workshops, and following, there was unanimous agreement that the time had arrived for some form of character education to be put back into the classroom. In contrast to the sentiments of the 1960s or 1970s, there seemed to be a strong feeling by superintendents and board members that, in addition to basic academic skills, there was now a tremendous opportunity for assisting youngsters to develop character traits that would help them become more effective parents, employees, and citizens.[25]

THE CHARACTER EDUCATION CURRICULUM

Increasing interest in the American Institute for Character Education's Character Education Curriculum provides additional evidence that the pendulum is swinging back toward character and ethics.

The curriculum is now used in more than seven thousand classrooms across the country. It has been approved by curriculum evaluation committees in many major cities, including Chicago, Denver, Los Angeles, Miami, New Orleans, New York, and Pittsburgh.

In Chicago, Superintendent Ruth Love has recommended, and the Chicago City Board of Education has agreed, that if it can be funded from outside sources, the Character Education Curriculum should be in every Chicago elementary school.

COLLEGE-LEVEL ETHICS COURSES

Although the emphasis in this book is on the primary and secondary levels, interest in ethics is also increasing at the college level.

Derek Bok, president of Harvard University and former Law School dean, recently made the following comments on the subject:

Universities have gone much too far in trying to produce value-free teaching and research. This happened primarily because scholars within universities were deluded by the thought that only completely objective, "scientific" inquiry was respectable and that values were not amenable to rigorous scholarship. . . . Many scholars even distorted the reality they studied in order to make it susceptible to their "rigorous" methods of analysis. . . .

Fortunately, there is now a movement to introduce values into the curriculum through courses in applied ethics that ask students to come to grips with significant ethical problems.[26]

The Hastings Center, a private research institution in New York, conducted a two-year survey of the teaching of ethics in colleges and universities. "Interest in applied and professional ethics has been spreading rapidly in higher education," according to Daniel Callahan, director of the center.

He said that ethics was central to the entire college curriculum in the nineteenth century, but in the twentieth century virtually no courses were offered outside departments of religion and philosophy.

Late in the 1960s the picture began to change. At the undergraduate level, the Hastings study found that the largest increase in ethics courses had taken place in the "hard" sciences. Ethical questions were also introduced more and more in humanities courses.

In contrast, according to the Hastings Center report, only a handful of social science programs dealt with ethics. "There seems to be outright hostility to giving ethics a place in graduate social science curricula," Callahan stated.

He said that most scholars agreed that ethics is important but were not convinced that it could be put into the curricula and taught in a systematic way.[27]

CENTURY III FOUNDATION

Arthur Melvin, founder and executive director of Century III Foundation, is one scholar who is convinced that young people and adults can be helped to clarify their basic values. Dr. Melvin, with the assistance of his wife, Marian, and their nine intellectually active children, has been testing ways to clarify values since 1966.

More than six thousand people have completed the foundation's three-day Value Analysis Workshop.[28] Participants are asked to discuss and reflect on a series of ethical questions such as:

> *Each human being:*
> *Is extraordinarily unique.*
> *Desires to be of good will.*
> *Searches for meaning.*
> *Desires to make his own choices.*
> *Has the ability to be rational.*
> *Desires well-being.*
> *Has a will which can affect the direction/flow of energy.*
> *Influences the quality of life by his behavior.[29]*

Those who have attended Value Analysis Workshops represent various education, career, economic, and political backgrounds and range from ten to eighty years in age. But interestingly, after three days of discussion and reflection, a remarkably high percentage of the workshop participants have reached consensus on fundamental personal and social ethical concepts.

Dr. Melvin provides impressive statistical data to support his statement that "over the past 15 years, Century III Foundation's research has revealed replicable, scientific evidence that 80 to 90 percent of people, self-identified by almost every possible label, upon reflection and interaction on the logical consequences of adequate alternatives, agree that a common moral standard does exist."[30]

"The data," states Melvin, "reveal evidence of a latent morality paradigm potentially available for use by and commonly resident within each person."[31]

Chapter 11

IN SUMMARY

More than two thousand years ago Plato warned: "If man's education is inadequate or bad, he becomes the most savage of all the products of earth."

The explosive increase in crime, violence, vandalism, drug abuse, youthful suicide, and other costly human problems clearly indicates that our society is failing in the crucial area of character education.

Most Americans do not know that our schools, before about 1910, gave ethical instruction a high priority, nor do they know that this emphasis has been greatly reduced.

The purpose of this book is to provide its readers with information to show that systematic ethical instruction in our schools is traditional, neglected, legal, feasible, and highly beneficial to everyone. All successful societies have recognized the importance of teaching their young people to be responsible.

Clearly, ethical instruction cannot be left to schools alone. Parents must be helped and encouraged to do a better job, as must churches, the media, and other key institutions. It would be marvelous if parents would train all of their children to be self-reliant, ethical, and responsible, but the fact is that many parents cannot or do not do so.

The school system, as Secretary of Education Terrel Bell has so correctly stated, "stands alone in having both the opportunity and the right to...assume the responsibility for moral education."

Fortunately, professional awareness of and interest in systematic ethical instruction are growing, and considerable

141

evidence now exists that the educational pendulum is swinging in the direction of such instruction.

The future health of our society depends upon a greatly renewed effort to create, test, and distribute workable programs to assist parents, schools, churches, and other institutions in helping young people develop sound character.

The need is urgent. The time is now. For, as Edmund Burke warned two centuries ago, "All that is necessary for the triumph of evil is for good men to do nothing."

NOTES

PREFACE

1. Warren E. Burger, *Annual Report to the American Bar Association,* Houston, February 8, 1981.

2. Terrel H. Bell, address at 18th Anniversary Banquet of Thomas Jefferson Research Center, November 17, 1981.

3. *The Writings of Thomas Jefferson,* ed. Paul Leicester Ford, 10 vols. (New York: G. P. Putnam's Sons, 1892–99), 9:227.

4. Benjamin Franklin, *The Writings of Benjamin Franklin,* ed. Albert Henry Smyth, 10 vols. (New York: Macmillan Co., 1905–7), 9:569.

5. "National Education Association Research Memo," NEA Research Division of the National Education Association, Washington, D.C., November 1963.

6. "Common Sense & Everyday Ethics," Ethics Resource Center, (division of American Viewpoint, Inc.), Washington, D.C., 1980.

7. M. G. Bowden, ed., "The Character-Education Project, Statement of Purposes and Plans," Bulletin no. 2 (San Antonio: Children's Fund, 1969), p. 2.

8. Edward A. Wynne, *Character II* 1, no. 4 (published by Character, Inc., Chicago) (July/August 1982).

CHAPTER 1

1. "The Children of Milpitas," *Modesto Bee,* December 10, 1981.

2. "Troubled Teenagers," *U.S. News & World Report,* December 14, 1981, p. 40.

3. James S. Coleman, news release by Character, Inc., Chicago, December 7, 1981.

4. Socrates, quoted in *Education in Upheaval* 21, no. 18.

5. Louis Honig, Jr., "Balancing the Curriculum," *California School Boards,* April/May 1980, p. 22.

6. Joseph A. Califano, Jr., in transmitting a report to Congress, January 1978.

7. U.S., Department of Health, Education, and Welfare, *Violent Schools—Safe Schools: The Safe School Study Report to the Congress,* vol. 1, (Washington, D.C.: National Institute of Education, January 1978), pp. 2, 32.

8. William H. Blanchard, "Coping with Man's Violence," *Los Angeles Times,* April 16, 1972.

9. *To Establish Justice, to Insure Domestic Tranquility,* final report on Causes and Prevention of Violence, Washington, D.C., December, 1969, p. xxi.

10. David Bazelon, speech to Western Society of Criminology, 1981.

11. Arthur Shenfield, "The Failure of Socialism, Learning from the Swedes and English," *Critical Issues* (Washington, D.C.: Heritage Foundation, 1980), pp. 19, 20.

12. John A. Howard, "The Proper Role of Moral Values in a Philosophy of Education," *Widening Horizons* 11, no. 1 (Rockford College, Rockford, Ill.) (September 1974).

13. Warren E. Burger, *Annual Report to the American Bar Association,* Houston, February 8, 1981.

14. Walter Lippmann, "Education Versus Western Civilization," address at annual meeting of American Association

for the Advancement of Science, December 29, 1940. In *American Scholar* (Spring 1941).

15. Honig, op. cit.

16. Steven Muller, "Universities Are Turning Out Highly Skilled Barbarians," *U.S. News & World Report,* November 10, 1980, p. 57.

17. John R. Silber, "The Gods of the Copy Book Headings: Reflections on the No-Fault Life," address at 17th Anniversary Banquet of Thomas Jefferson Research Center, November 25, 1980.

18. George C. Roche III, "Truly Private Education," *Imprimis* 7, no. 10 (Hillsdale College, Hillsdale, Mich.) (October 1978).

19. John A. Howard, "Rediscovering Joy," Bohemian Grove Lakeside Talk, July 24, 1973, p. 3.

20. George C. S. Benson and Thomas S. Engeman, *Amoral America* (1975; rev. ed., Durham, N.C.: Carolina Academic Press, 1982).

21. Ibid., pp. 27, 224, 225.

22. Mark W. Cannon, "Crime and the Decline of Values," speech to Southwestern Judicial Conference, Santa Fe, N.M., June 4, 1981.

CHAPTER 2

1. Sandrah L. Pohorlak, "The Status of the Teaching of Moral and Spiritual Values in the Public Schools of the United States, Territories and Possessions" (Master's thesis, University of Southern California, 1967), pp. 13, 14.

2. Edwin F. Klotz, "Guidelines for Moral Instruction in California Schools," California State Department of Education, May 9, 1969.

3. George C. S. Benson and Thomas S. Engeman, *Amoral America* (1975; rev. ed., Durham, N.C.: Carolina Academic Press, 1982), pp. 23, 24

145

4. Ibid.

5. Ibid., p. 11.

6. Ibid., pp. 186, 187.

7. Richard de Charms and Gerald H. Moeller, "Values Expressed in American Children's Readers, 1800–1950," *Journal of Abnormal and Social Psychology* 64 (1962): 136–42.

8. Margaret P. Foster, "A Study of the Content of Selected Third Grade Basic Readers Used in the United States from 1900 to 1953" (Master's thesis, Wesleyan University, Conn., 1956).

9. Harry C. McKown, *Character Education* (New York: McGraw-Hill, 1935), p. 74.

10. John Nietz, *Evolution of American Secondary School Texts* (Rutland, Vt.: C. Tuttle, 1966).

11. Augustin G. Rudd, *Bending the Twig,* (Chicago: Heritage Foundation, 1957), p. 167.

12. Abraham H. Maslow, *Religions, Values and Peak Experiences* (Columbus: Ohio State University Press, 1965).

13. Walter Lippmann, "Education Versus Western Civilization," address at annual meeting of American Association for the Advancement of Science, December 19, 1940.

14. John Jarolimek, "But Who Bends the Twig?" *Character Education Journal* 2, no. 2 (Winter 1973):15.

15. Louis Honig, Jr., "Balancing the Curriculum," *California School Boards,* April/May 1980, p. 22.

16. *National Education Association Journal* (January 1967).

17. Benjamin D. Wood, memorandum to Frank Goble, July 23, 1966.

18. Terrel H. Bell, address at 18th Anniversary Banquet of Thomas Jefferson Research Center, November 17, 1981.

19. Klotz, op cit., p. 7.

20. M. Donald Thomas and Rafael Lewy, "Education and Moral Conduct: Re-Discovering America," *Character* 1, no. 4 (January 1980).

21. Lawrence Kohlberg, "Teaching Virtues," *Ethical Education* (Winter 1971).

22. David Elton Trueblood, *General Philosophy* (New York: Harper & Row, 1963), p. 261.

23. Louis E. Raths, "What I Believe About Character Education," *Character Education Journal* (Fall 1972).

24. Louis E. Raths, Merrill Harmin, and Sidney B. Simon, *Values and Teaching: Working with Values in the Classroom* (Columbus, Ohio: Charles E. Merrill Books), pp. 10, 47.

25. Benson and Engeman, op. cit., p. 18.

26. Ibid.

27. Ibid., p. 19.

28. Page Smith, "'Cogito Ergo Sum'—And Then Came Watergate," *Los Angeles Times,* June 11, 1973.

29. Jacqueline Bouhoutsos, "Science and Movies Face Same Dilemma," *Los Angeles Times,* April 26, 1970.

30. Louis Honig, Jr., "The Forgotten Case for Virtue," 1978.

CHAPTER 3

1. Thomas D. Haire, "Street Gangs: Some Suggested Remedies for Violence and Vandalism," *Police Chief* (Los Angeles), July 1979, p. 55.

2. Sheldon and Eleanor Glueck, "A Decade of Research in Criminology: Stock-taking and a Forward Look," address at Annual Banquet of Harvard Voluntary Defenders, Harvard University, April 15, 1963. Reprinted from *Excerpta Criminologica* 3, no. 5 (September/October 1963).

3. "Why Young People 'Go Bad,'" exclusive interview with Professor and Mrs. Sheldon Glueck of Harvard Law School, *U.S. News & World Report,* April 26, 1965, p. 56.

4. Sheldon and Eleanor Glueck, "Delinquents and Nondelinquents in Depressed Areas: Some Guidelines for Community Action," *Community Mental Health Journal* 2, no. 3 (Fall 1966):218.

5. "Children of Permissive Parents Most Likely to Take Drugs, Research Reveals," *National Enquirer,* October 1, 1972.

6. Paul Roazen, *Freud: Political and Social Thought* (New York: Alfred A. Knopf, 1968), p. 103.

7. Richard H. Blum & Associates, *Horatio Alger's Children: The Role of the Family in the Origin and Prevention of Drug Risk* (San Francisco: Jossey-Bass, 1972), pp. 59–61.

8. Ibid., p. 305.

9. "Opinion Roundup," *Public Opinion* 2, no. 2 (American Enterprise Institute for Public Policy Research, Washington, D.C.) (March/May 1979):36.

10. George C. S. Benson and Thomas S. Engeman, *Amoral America* (1975; rev. ed., Durham, N.C.: Carolina Academic Press, 1982), pp. 182, 183.

11. John F. Travers and Russell G. Davis, "A Study of Religious Motivation and Delinquency," *Journal of Educational Sociology* 20 (January 1961).

12. Fredric Wertham, "School for Violence, Mayhem in the Mass Media," in *Where Do You Draw the Line?* ed. Victor B. Cline (Provo, Utah: Brigham Young University Press, 1974), p. 157. Reprinted by permission.

13. Ibid., p. 161.

14. "What Is TV Doing to America?" *U.S. News & World Report,* August 2, 1982, p. 27.

15. Ibid.

16. Wertham, op. cit., pp. 164, 173, 174.

17. Sandrah L. Pohorlak, "The Status of the Teaching of Moral and Spiritual Values in the Public Schools of the United States, Territories and Possessions" (Master's thesis, University of Southern California, 1967), pp. 13, 14.

18. Mark W. Cannon, "The Critical Role of Principals in Strengthening Society's Value System," *NASSP bulletin* 65, no. 448 (Reston, Va.) (November 1981):82.

19. Richard Gorsuch, "Teacher and Pupil Values in the Elementary Schools," *Character Education Journal* (Fall 1972):20.

20. U. Bronfenbrenner, *Two Worlds of Childhood* (New York: Russell Sage, 1970).

21. Ellwood P. Cubberley, *Public Education in the United States* (1947).

22. John Dewey, *Democracy and Education* (New York: Free Press, 1966), p. 359.

23. Edwin F. Klotz, "Guidelines for Moral Instruction in California Schools," California State Department of Education, May 9, 1969, p. 24.

24. Pohorlak, op. cit., p. 12.

25. "National Education Association Research Memo," NEA Research Division of the National Education Association, Washington, D.C., November 1963.

26. Ibid.

27. Pohorlak, op. cit.

28. Terrel H. Bell, address at 18th Anniversary Banquet of Thomas Jefferson Research Center, November 17, 1981.

CHAPTER 4

1. Edwin F. Klotz, "Guidelines for Moral Instruction in California Schools," California State Department of Education, May 9, 1969, p. 5.

2. Herbert C. Mayer, "The Good American Program—A Teacher's Guide to the Direct Teaching of Citizenship Values in the Elementary Grades" (New York: American Viewpoint, 1964).

3. Sheldon and Eleanor Glueck, *Delinquency in the Making* (New York: Harper & Row, 1952).

4. H. Hartshorne, M. A. May, and F. K. Shuttleworth, *Studies in the Organization of Character* (New York: Macmillan Co., 1930).

5. Robert F. Peck with Robert J. Havighurst and Ruth Cooper, Jesse Lilienthal, and Douglas More, *The Psychology of Character Development,* (New York: John Wiley & Sons, 1960), p. 189.

6. Gene L. Schwilck, "An Experimental Study of the Effectiveness of Direct and Indirect Methods of Character Education," *Studies in Character Research* 1, no. 14 (Union College Character Education Project, Schenectady, N.Y.) (May 1956).

7. Virginia Trevitt, *The American Heritage: Design for National Character* (Santa Barbara, Calif: McNally & Loftin, 1965).

8. Virginia Trevitt, "Challenge Youth in the Space Age," address given at Bloomfield Hills, Mich., undated.

9. This example is condensed from an article by Dorothy Kobak, "Teaching Children to Care," *Jefferson Research Letter,* no. 115, October 1975.

10. This section is condensed from an article by Edward F. Haskell, "Building Character in a Harlem School," *Jefferson Research Letter,* no. 162, September 1979. Professor Haskell is chairman of the Council for Unified Research and Education.

11. Beatrice Bowles to Dr. Patricia Graham, Character Education Project, San Antonio, April 2, 1971.

12. Beatrice Bowles, "Public School #63: A Follow-up Report," April 1976.

13. Michael Martin, speech at Curriculum Conference of the Association of School Administrators, San Diego, October 13–14, 1978.

14. H.C. Mayer to American Institute for Character Education, April 25, 1978.

15. Principal, John J. Pershing Elementary School, San Antonio, from film, *From Classroom to Community,* produced by American Institute for Character Education, San Antonio, 1981.

16. Lawrence H. James to Director of Instruction, Los Angeles Unified School District, April 1, 1981.

17. Jim W. Casey to American Institute for Character Education, January 10, 1980.

18. Mattie Adderly, second-grade teacher, quoted in letter to Y. Jay Mulkey from William R. Renuart, Dade County, Fla., October 13, 1980.

19. James C. Enochs, "The Restoration of Standards: The Modesto Plan" (Bloomington, Ind.: Phi Delta Kappa Educational Foundation, 1979), pp. 7, 8, 9.

20. Ibid., pp. 19–24.

21. Ibid.

22. James C. Enochs to Frank Goble, April 1, 1981.

23. Lee Cronbach, *Educational Psychology* (New York: Harcourt, Brace, 1954).

24. William Glasser, *Reality Therapy—A New Approach to Psychiatry* (New York: Harper & Row, 1965), p. 43.

25. Ibid.

26. Ibid., pp. xv, 67.

27. Alfred A. Montapert, *Distilled Wisdom* (Englewood Cliffs, N.J.: Prentice-Hall, 1964), p. 26.

28. Luciano L'Abate, "An Evaluation of Emotional Maturity Instruction: A Review of Assumptions, Methods, and Results," April 1, 1974.

29. John Fisher, "Emotional Maturity Instruction Recidivism, Dougherty Juvenile Court," Albany, Ga., November 15, 1977.

30. Carl Schmidt, "A Research Proposal for Evaluating the Effectiveness of Emotional Maturity Instruction" (Unpublished Ph.D. thesis, Florida State University, 1979).

31. Jerry D. Hill, Report to Director, Community Responsibility Training Unit, San Bernardino, Calif., March 29, 1982.

CHAPTER 5

1. Edwin F. Klotz, "Guidelines for Moral Instruction in California Schools," California State Department of Education, May 9, 1969, p. 72.

2. David Lawrence, "Teaching of Morality Has Not Been Tabooed," *U.S. News & World Report,* February 13, 1967, p. 112.

3. Stephen Arons, "The Separation of School and State: *Pierce* Reconsidered," *Harvard Educational Review* 46, no. 1 (February 1976).

4. George B. de Huszar, Henry W. Littlefield, and Arthur W. Littlefield, eds., *Basic American Documents* (Ames, Iowa: Littlefield, Adams, 1953), p. 66.

5. *The Writings of Thomas Jefferson,* ed. Paul Leicester Ford, 10 vols. (New York: G. P. Putnam's Sons, 1892–99):227.

6. Jonathan Elliot, ed., *The Debates in the Several State Conventions in the Adoption of the Federal Constitution,* 5 vols. (Philadelphia: J. B. Lippincott, 1901), 3:536–37.

7. William V. Wells, *The Life and Public Services of Samuel Adams,* 3 vols. (Boston: Brown & Company, 1865), 3:175.

8. Adrienne Koch, ed., *The American Enlightenment* (New York: George Braziller, 1965), p. 77.

9. Values Education Commission, Maryland, "Statement of Purpose," July 30, 1979.

10. Stephen H. Sachs, Report to Values Education Commission, Maryland, July 1979.

11. Daniel Callahan and Sissela Bok, "The Role of Applied Ethics in Learning," *Change* (Hildref Publications, Washington, D.C.) (September 1979).

12. Terrel H. Bell, speech at National Conference for Education and Citizenship, Kansas City, Mo., September 23, 1976; reprinted in *Jefferson Research Letter,* no. 134, May 1977.

13. State of California Education Code, Section 44806, "Duty Concerning Instruction of Pupils Concerning Morals, Manners and Citizenship."

14. Michigan State Board of Education, "Resolution," March 13, 1968.

15. Michigan State Board of Eduation, "Resolution on Moral Values and Value Systems," August 28, 1968.

16. Sandrah L. Pohorlak, "The Status of the Teaching of Moral and Spiritual Values in the Public Schools of the United States, Territories and Possessions" (Master's thesis, University of Southern California, 1967), p. 21.

17. Virginia, Legislature, *House Joint Resolution No. 303,* February 8, 1981.

CHAPTER 6

1. Andrew Oldenquist, "'Indoctrination' and Societal Suicide," *Public Interest,* no. 63 (Spring 1981):81.

2. *U.S. News & World Report,* March 4, 1968.

3. W. D. Humbly, "Origins of Education Among Primitive Peoples, 1926," cited in Frederick Eby and Charles Flinn Arrowood, *The History and Philosophy of Education Ancient and Medieval* (1940), p. 15.

4. Ibid., p. 17.

5. Ibid., pp. 87f.

6. *For Thinkers on Education* (Mylapore, Madras: Sri Ramakrishna Math, 1948), bk. 1, pp. 3; xi.

7. Plato, *Protagoras.*

8. Elizabeth Seeger, *The Pageant of Chinese History* (1962), p. 45.

9. J. Eric Thompson, *Mexico Before Cortez* (New York: Charles Scribner's Sons, 1933).

10. Eby and Arrowood, op. cit., p. 578.

11. F. A. P. Barnard, 1872, as cited in Ellwood P. Cubberley, *Public Education in the United States* (1947), pp. 33f.

12. Irving Babbitt, *Democracy and Leadership* (Boston: Houghton Mifflin Co., 1924), p. 303.

13. Cubberley, op. cit., p. 41.

14. Reed J. Irvine, "Why Not Try Teaching Moral Precepts Again," *Sunday Star* (Washington, D.C.), April 9. 1967.

15. Lenore Romney, meeting sponsored by National Center for Voluntary Action, Frederick, Md., May 16, 1972.

16. Maurice Connery, "DUI Tieline," DUI Demonstration Program funded by California Office of Traffic Safety, no. 6, January 1980, p. 3.

17. John R. Silber, "The Gods of the Copy Book Headings: Reflections on the No-Fault Life," address at 17th Anniversary Banquet of Thomas Jefferson Research Center, November 25, 1980.

18. George C. S. Benson and Thomas S. Engeman, *Amoral America* (1975; rev. ed., Durham, N.C.: Carolina Academic Press, 1982), p. 25.

CHAPTER 7

1. Philip H. Phenix, "The Moral Imperative in Contemporary American Education," *Perspectives on Education* (Teachers College, Columbia University) (Winter 1969):7.

2. Lewis Mayhew, from address given when he became president of Association of Higher Education.

3. Los Angeles Unified School District, Instructional Planning Division, *The Teaching of Values,* Publication no. GC-56, 1978.

4. Benjamin Franklin, *The Writings of Benjamin Franklin,* ed. Albert Henry Smyth, 10 vols. (New York: Macmillan Co., 1905–7), 9:569.

5. Norman Cousins, ed., *In God We Trust* (New York: Harper Brothers, 1959), pp. 420, 439.

6. Declaration of Independence.

7. Carl L. Becker, *Freedom and Responsibility in the American Way of Life* (New York: Alfred A. Knopf, 1955), p. 52.

8. Robert M. Hutchins, *The Human Dialogue,* p. 322.

9. Robert F. Peck with Robert J. Havighurst, et al., *The Psychology of Character Development* (New York: John Wiley & Sons, 1960), p. 199.

10. Abraham H. Maslow, "Some Education Implications of the Humanistic Psychologies," *Harvard Educational Review* (Fall 1968):1.

11. Abraham H. Maslow, "Music Education and Peak-Experiences," *Music Educators Journal* (1968).

12. Abraham H. Maslow, *The Psychology of Science* (New York: Harper & Row, 1966), p. 133.

13. Abraham H. Maslow, "Fusions of Facts and Values," *American Journal of Psychoanalysis* (Brandeis University) (1963):23.

CHAPTER 8

1. Character Education Task Force, "A Reawakening: Character Education and the Role of the School Board Member," California School Boards Association, August 1982, pp. 2, 3.

2. Task Force Report on *Student Violence & Vandalism,* California School Boards Association, September 1980, p. 4.

3. Character Education Task Force, op. cit., p. 4.

4. Herbert C. Mayer, "The Good American Program—A Teacher's Guide to the Direct Teaching of Citizenship Values in the Elementary Grades" (New York: American Viewpoint, 1964).

5. Ibid., p. 14.

6. Ibid., p. 3.

7. Virginia Trevitt, *The American Heritage,* op. cit.

8. John R. Silber, "The Gods of the Copy Book Headings: Reflections on the No-Fault Life," address at 17th Anniversary Banquet of Thomas Jefferson Research Center, November 25, 1980.

9. Joseph Forcinelli and Thomas S. Engeman, "Value Education in the Public School," *Thrust* (Journal of Association of California School Administrators (October 1974):15.

10. George C. S. Benson and Thomas S. Engeman, *Amoral America* (1975; rev. ed., Durham, N.C.: Carolina Academic Press, 1982), p. 175.

11. Ibid., pp. 175, 176.

12. Reed J. Irvine, "Why Not Try Teaching Moral Precepts Again," *Sunday Star* (Washington, D.C.), April 9, 1967.

13. William J. Bennett and Edwin J. Delattre, "Moral Education in the Schols," *Public Interest* (Winter 1978):82.

14. Ibid.

15. Ibid., p. 83.

16. Ibid.

17. Ibid., p. 85.

18. Ibid.

19. Lawrence Kohlberg, "Stages of Moral Development as a Basis for Moral Education," *Moral Education: Interdisciplinary Approaches,* ed. Clive Beck et al. (Toronto: University of Toronto Press, 1971), p. 71.

20. Lawrence Kohlberg and E. Turiel, *Moralization Research, the Cognitive-Developmental Approach* (New York: Holt, Rinehart, & Winston, 1975).

21. Kathleen M. Gow, *Yes, Virginia, There Is Right and Wrong! Values Education Survival Kit* (Toronto: John Wiley & Sons Canada, 1980), p. 53.

22. Ibid.

23. Richard A. Baer, Jr., "Parents, Schools and Value Clarification," *Wall Street Journal,* April 12, 1982.

24. Reo M. Christenson, "Clarifying Values Clarification for the Innocent," *Christianity Today,* April 10, 1981, p. 3.

CHAPTER 9

1. Robert J. Cahill and H. W. Handy, "Character Education: Summative Evaluation of the First Generation Curriculum Developed by the American Institute for Character Education," American Institutes for Research, August 1974.

2. D. Jeanne Callihan and Bruce Frazee, "An Independent Evaluation of the Character Education Program in the Dade County Schools of Miami, Florida" San Antonio, 1979, American Institute for.Character Education.

3. Ibid.

4. Ibid., pp. 7, 9.

5. *AICE Newsletter* (American Institute for Character Education, San Antonio) (Spring 1983):2.

6. Jane Terry to American Institute for Character Education, April 3, 1978.

7. Michael Martin, speech at Curriculum Conference of the Association of School Administrators, San Diego, October 13–14, 1978.

8. Beatrice Bowles to Dr. Patricia Graham, Character Education Project, San Antonio, April 2, 1971.

9. AICE film, *"From Classroom to Community,"* 1981.

10. Beatrice Bowles, "Public School #63: A Follow-up Report," April 1976.

11. Jim Casey to AICE, January 10, 1980.

12. Lawrence H. James to Director of Instruction, Los Angeles Unified School District, April 1, 1981.

13. William R. Renuart, Principal, David Fairchild Elementary School, Miami, to Y. Jay Mulkey, President, American Institute for Character Education, 1982.

14. George H. Gallup, "The 13th Annual Gallup Poll of the Public's Attitudes Toward the Public Schools," *Phi Delta Kappan* (Bloomington, Ind.) (September 1981):39.

15. Solveig Eggerz, "Why Our Public Schools Are Failing and What We Must Do About It" (New Rochelle, N.Y.: America's Future, 1982).

16. Ibid.

17. Ibid., p. 19.

18. "Education in Values," American Enterprise Institute, p. 5.

19. Eggerz, op. cit.

20. *Dallas Times Herald,* September 26, 1982.

CHAPTER 10

1. Howard Flieger, "Newcomer on Campus," *U.S. News & World Report,* September 29, 1975, p. 92.

2. Marvin Stone, "Are Ethics on the Way Back?" *U.S. News & World Report,* January 22, 1979, p. 80.

3. George C. S. Benson and Thomas S. Engeman, *Amoral America* (1975; rev. ed., Durham, N.C.: Carolina Academic Press, 1982), p. 116.

4. Benson and Engeman, op. cit.

5. Terry Eastland, "Teaching Morality in the Public Schools," *Wall Street Journal,* February 22, 1982, p. 24.

6. Mark Blum, *Ethical-Citizenship Education Policies and Programs: A National Survey of State Education Agencies* (Research for Better Schools, Inc., Philadelphia) (Spring 1977).

7. Ibid., pp. 1, 3.

8. Task Force Report on *Student Violence & Vandalism,* California School Boards Association, September 1980, pp. 7, 8, 9.

9. Character Education Task Force, "A Reawakening: Character Education and the Role of the School Board Member," California School Boards Association, August 1982, p. ii.

10. Charles E. Bennett, Report to Subcommittee on Elementary, Secondary and Vocational Education, of the House Committee on Education and Labor, April 24, 1979.

11. Albert Rodda, "Character Education Hearing by Senate Select Committee on Innovations in School Finance and Character Education," State of California, Sacramento, September 24, 1980.

12. Bill AB399, California Assembly, Sacramento, June 25, 1981.

13. Values Education Commission, Maryland, "Statement of Purpose," July 30, 1979.

14. "Panel Wavers on How to Teach Values in Md. Public Schools," *Washington Post,* April 8, 1982.

15. "Education in Moral Values in Michigan," Michigan State Board of Education, 1967.

16. Ibid.

17. "Resolution on Moral Values and Value Systems," adopted by Michigan State Board of Education, August 28, 1968. See also Chapter 5 herein.

18. Memorandum from Donald G. Gill to Illinois State Board of Education's Planning and Policy Committee, December 3, 1981.

19. Donald G. Gill, "Project on Democratic Values," report to Illinois State Board of Education, December 3, 1981.

20. William J. Bennett, "Simple Truths—My Turn," *Newsweek,* January 7, 1980, p. 7.

21. Editorial, "Teach 3 Rs, Not 'Values,'" *Chicago Sun Times,* December 11, 1981, p. 63.

22. M. Donald Thomas, "Moral Education at South High School" (Salt Lake City), June 29, 1981.

23. Maryline White, "Character, Schools to Help Develop It," *Evening Express* (Portland, Maine), August 29, 1980, p. 16.

24. Peter R. Greer, "Another Simple Truth" (Portland, Maine), May 1982.

25. Thomas Jefferson Research Center, final report on "Values and Leadership Training for School Board Members, School District Superintendents and Principals," submitted to U.S. Department of Education, July 1982, p. 49.

26. Conversation with Derek Bok, "Students Need to Grapple with 'Significant Ethical Problems,'" *U.S. News & World Report,* February 21, 1983, p. 83.

27. Karen J. Winkler, "Sharp Increase Reported in Courses on Ethics," *Chronicle of Higher Education,* September 4, 1979.

28. M. Donald Thomas and Arthur I. Melvin, "Community Consensus Is Available on a Moral Valuing Standard," *Phi Delta Kappan* 62, no. 7 (March 1981).

29. "Discover a Common Sense Moral Standard in Value Analysis" (Oak Brook, Ill.: Century III Foundation, 1976), p. 13.

30. Arthur I. Melvin, "Scientific Evidence Reveals Agreement on a Common-Sense Moral Valuing Standard" (Oak Brook, Ill.: Century III Foundation).

31. Arthur I. Melvin, "Discovering Consensus on a Moral Valuing Standard: A Descriptive and Experimental Study of Century III's Valuing Analysis Process" (Ph.D. diss., Northwestern University, 1979).

INDEX

165

167

168

BIOGRAPHIES

Frank G. Goble is founder and president of the Thomas Jefferson Research Center in Pasadena, and former president of the D. B. Milliken Corporation. He left industry at the age of forty-six after a highly successful business career to devote full time to the work of the Center. Under his direction, the Center has conducted extensive interdisciplinary research in the social and behavioral sciences. He graduated from the University of California with highest scholastic honors and is a licensed mechanical engineer.

Mr. Goble is the author of three books, numerous articles and research reports, and three audio-cassette albums. He is a leading authority on the work of Abraham Maslow, and his book *The Third Force: The Psychology of Abraham Maslow* has been printed in four foreign languages and is widely used as a college reference text. His second book, *Excellence in Leadership,* was a 1973 selection for the American Management Association's "President's Bookshelf." His third book is *Beyond Failure: How to Cure a Neurotic Society.*

In addition to writing, Mr. Goble lectures and conducts workshops on leadership, motivation, and applied psychology.

B. David Brooks, Ph.D., is vice president of the Thomas Jefferson Research Center and heads the Center's Safe Schools Project. He writes, lectures, and conducts workshops on youth problems and has gained recognition as a leading authority on the subject.

While principal of John Glenn High School in Norwalk, California, he developed a highly successful program to control severe youth gang violence. Before that, Dr. Brooks had twelve years of experience as a teacher and school administrator. In 1980-81 he was director of the Biola Youth Services Project, providing remedial programs for inner-city youth gangs. His Ph.D. in human behavior was obtained from United States International University.